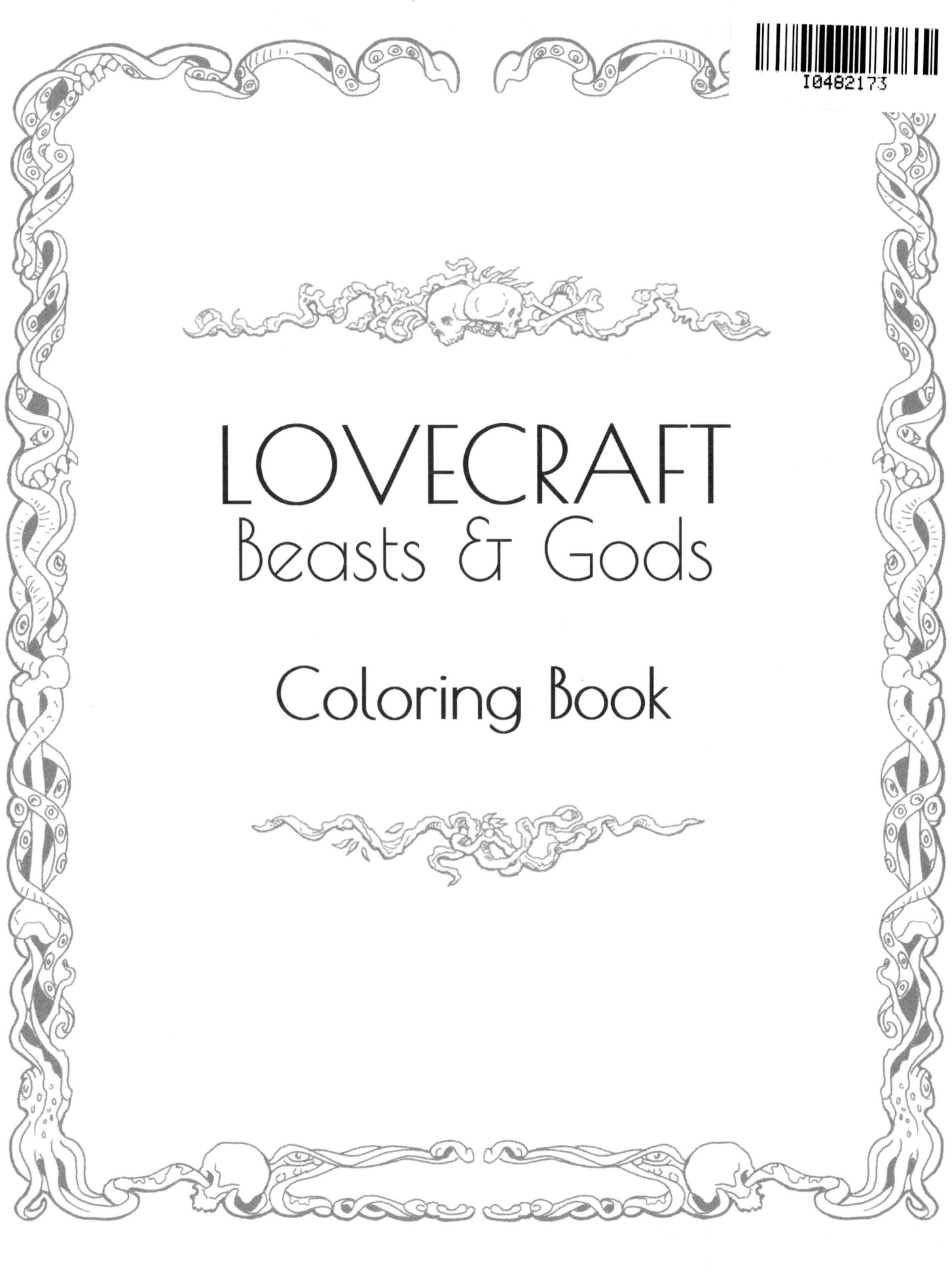

LOVECRAFT
Beasts & Gods

Coloring Book

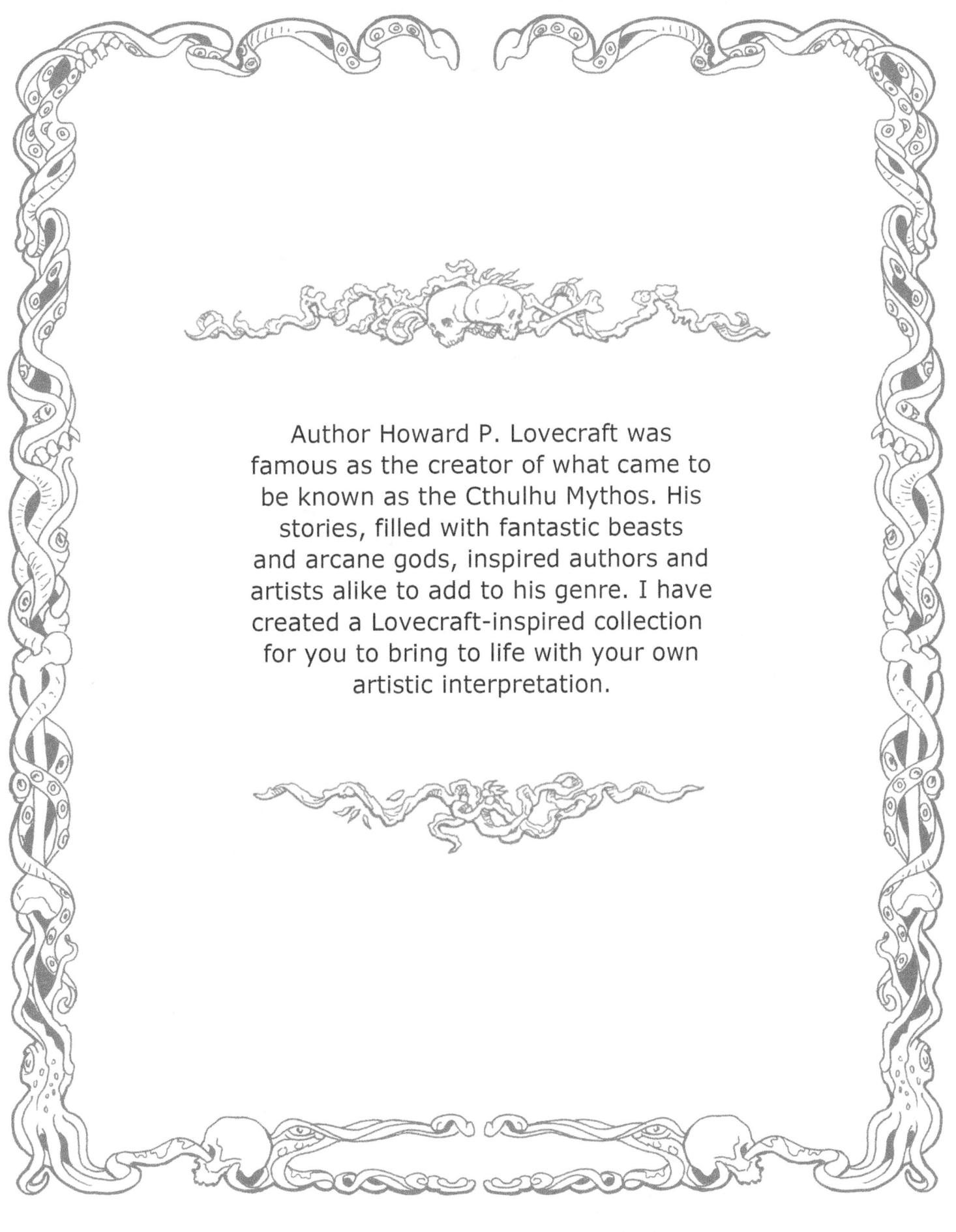

Author Howard P. Lovecraft was
famous as the creator of what came to
be known as the Cthulhu Mythos. His
stories, filled with fantastic beasts
and arcane gods, inspired authors and
artists alike to add to his genre. I have
created a Lovecraft-inspired collection
for you to bring to life with your own
artistic interpretation.

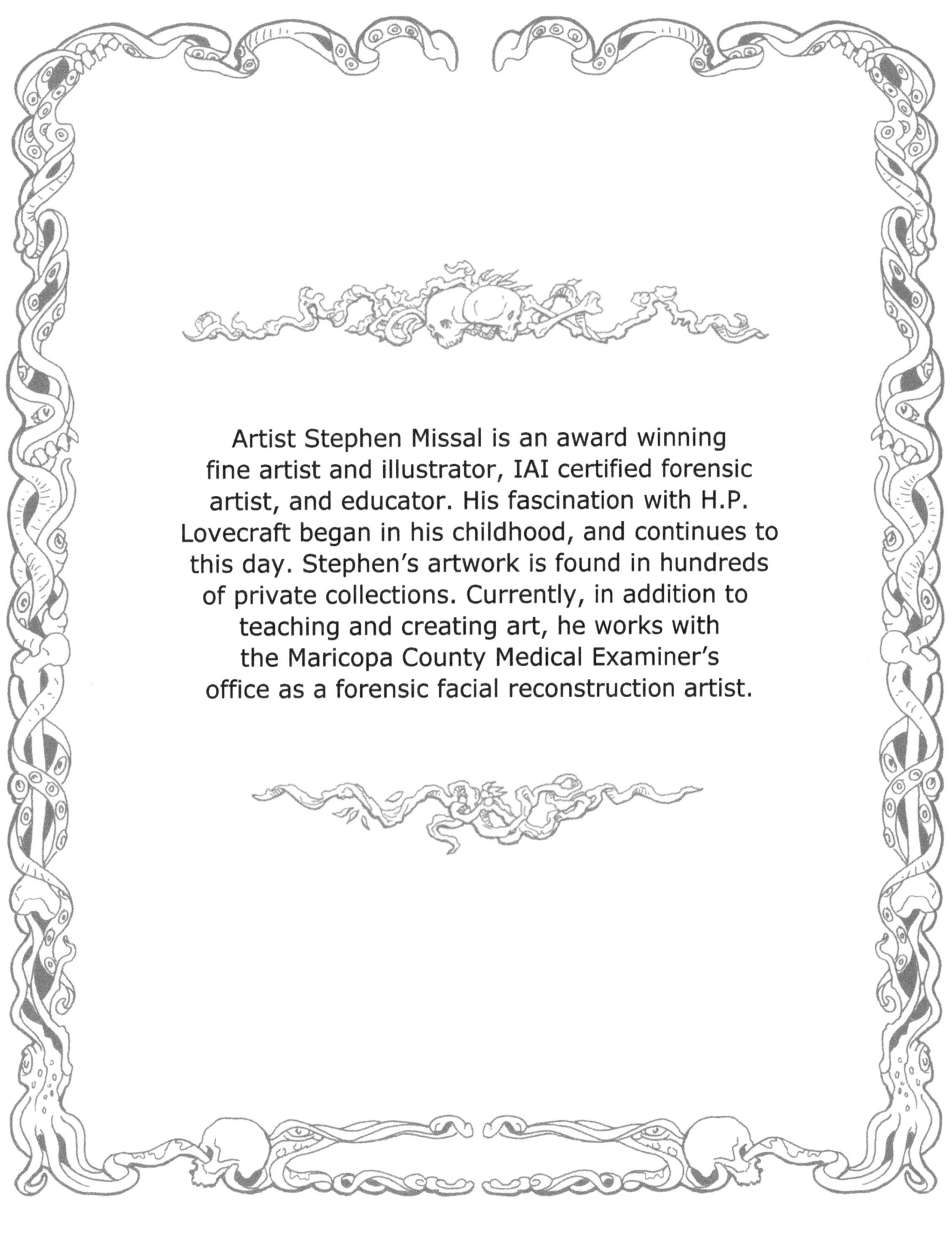

Artist Stephen Missal is an award winning
fine artist and illustrator, IAI certified forensic
artist, and educator. His fascination with H.P.
Lovecraft began in his childhood, and continues to
this day. Stephen's artwork is found in hundreds
of private collections. Currently, in addition to
teaching and creating art, he works with
the Maricopa County Medical Examiner's
office as a forensic facial reconstruction artist.

Atlach-Nacha

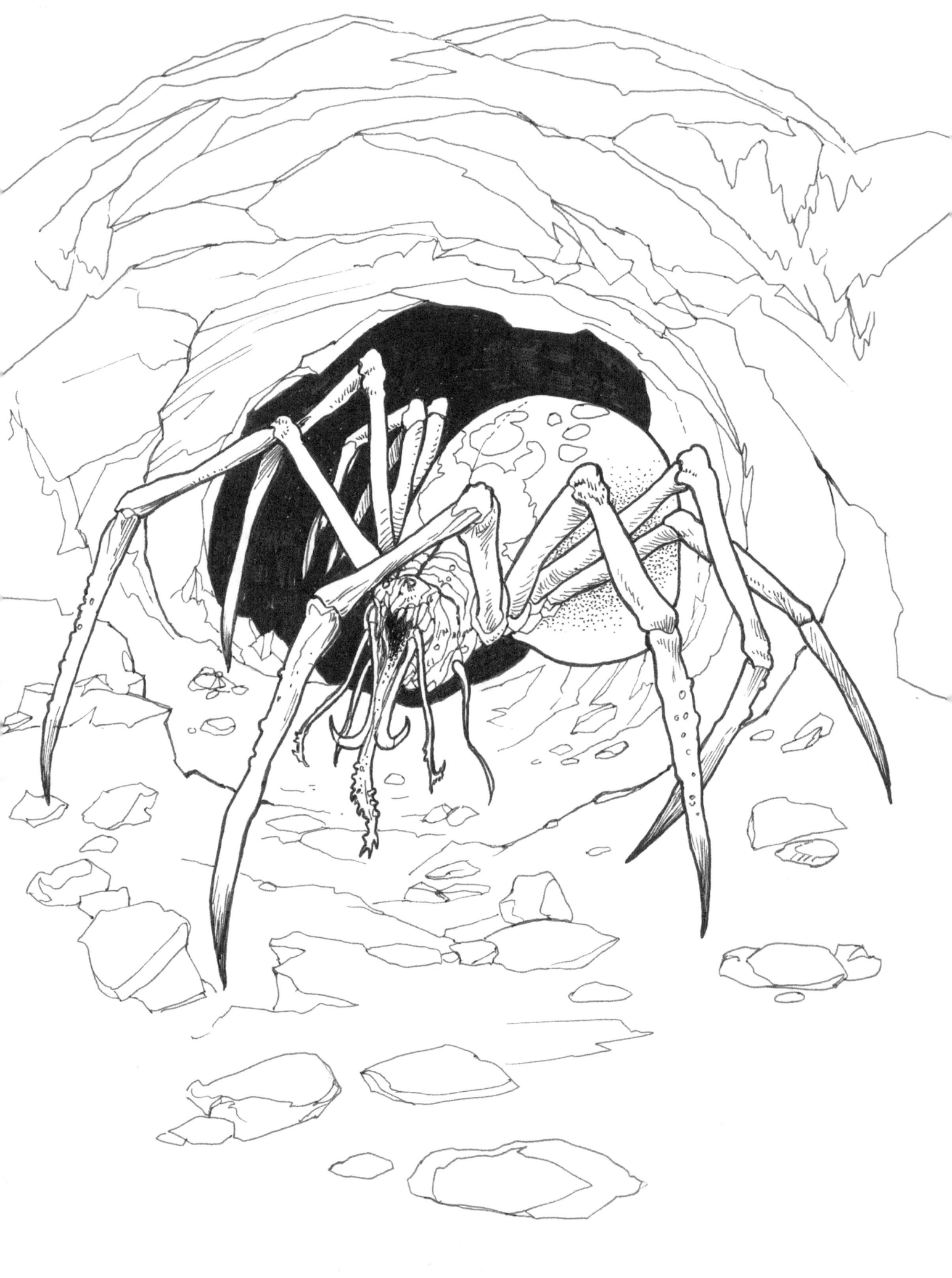

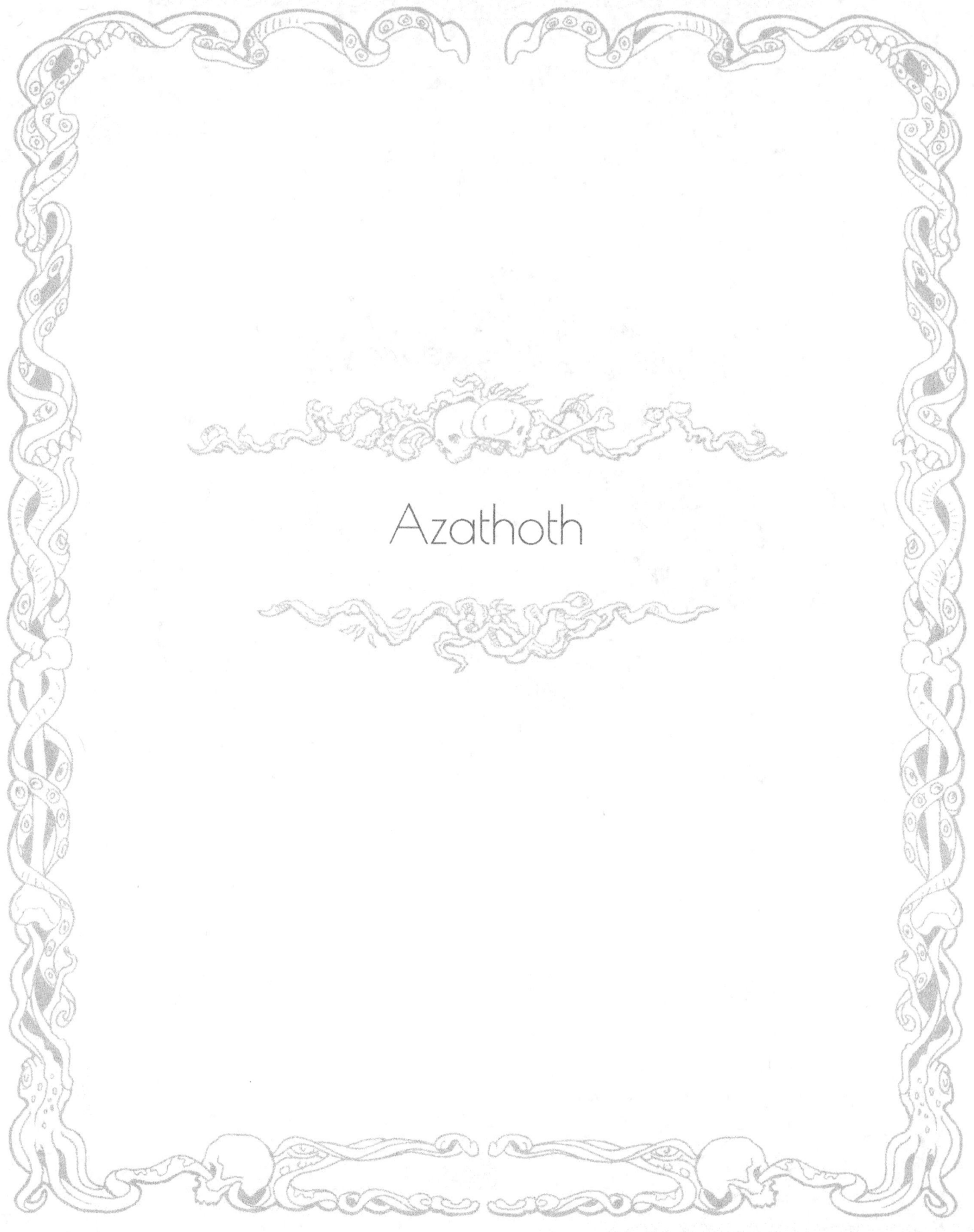

Azathoth

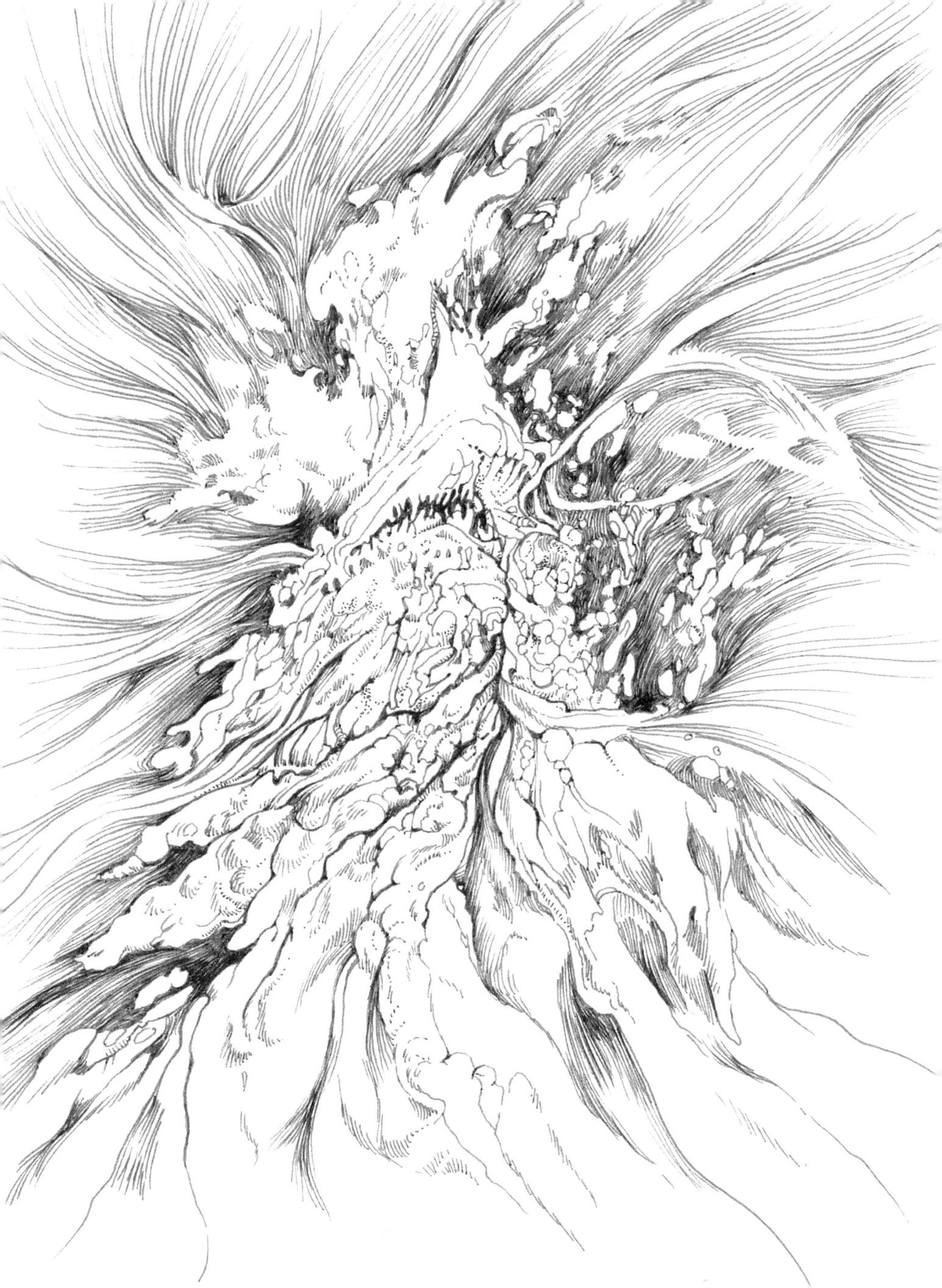

Brown Jenkin

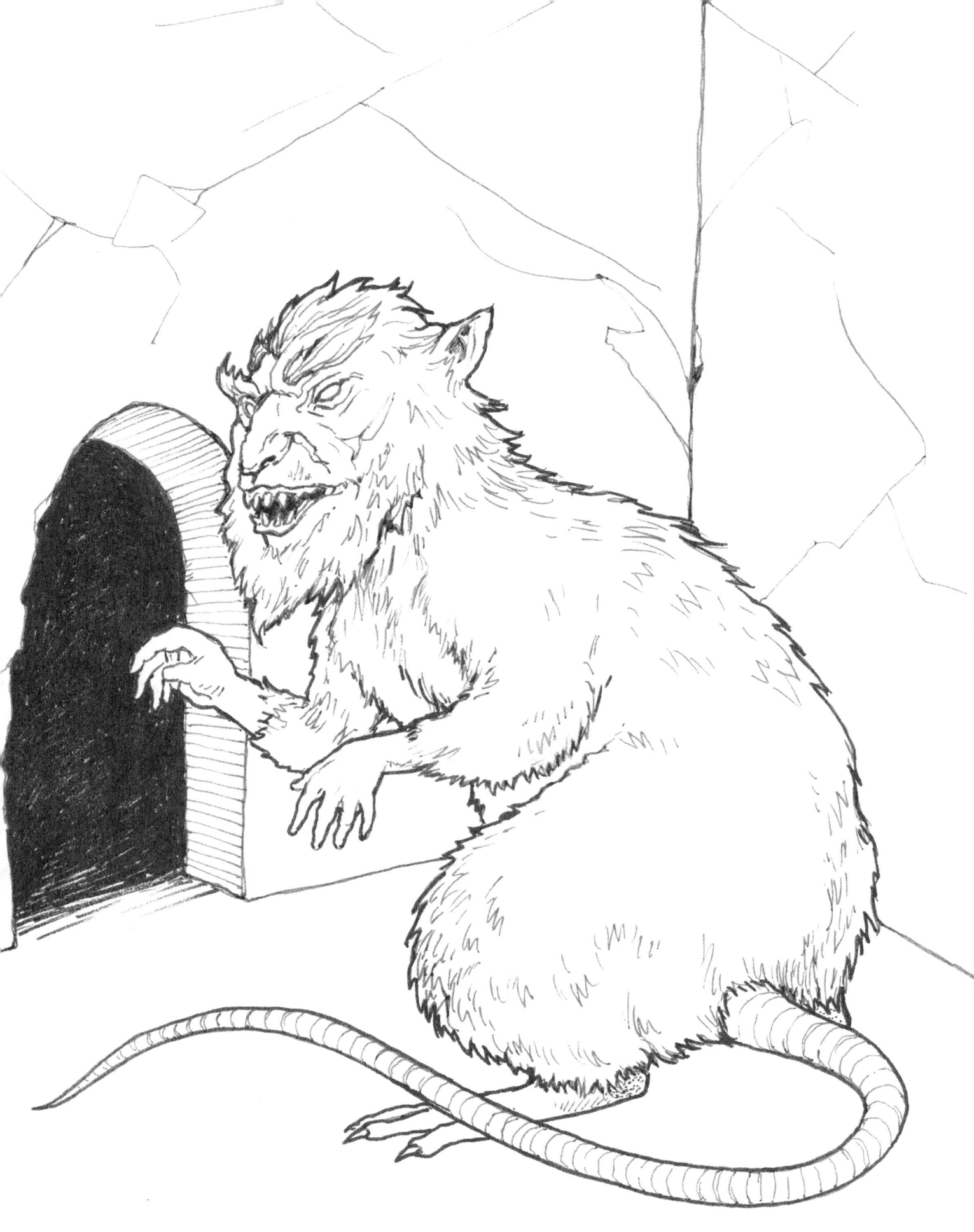

Chaugnar Faugn

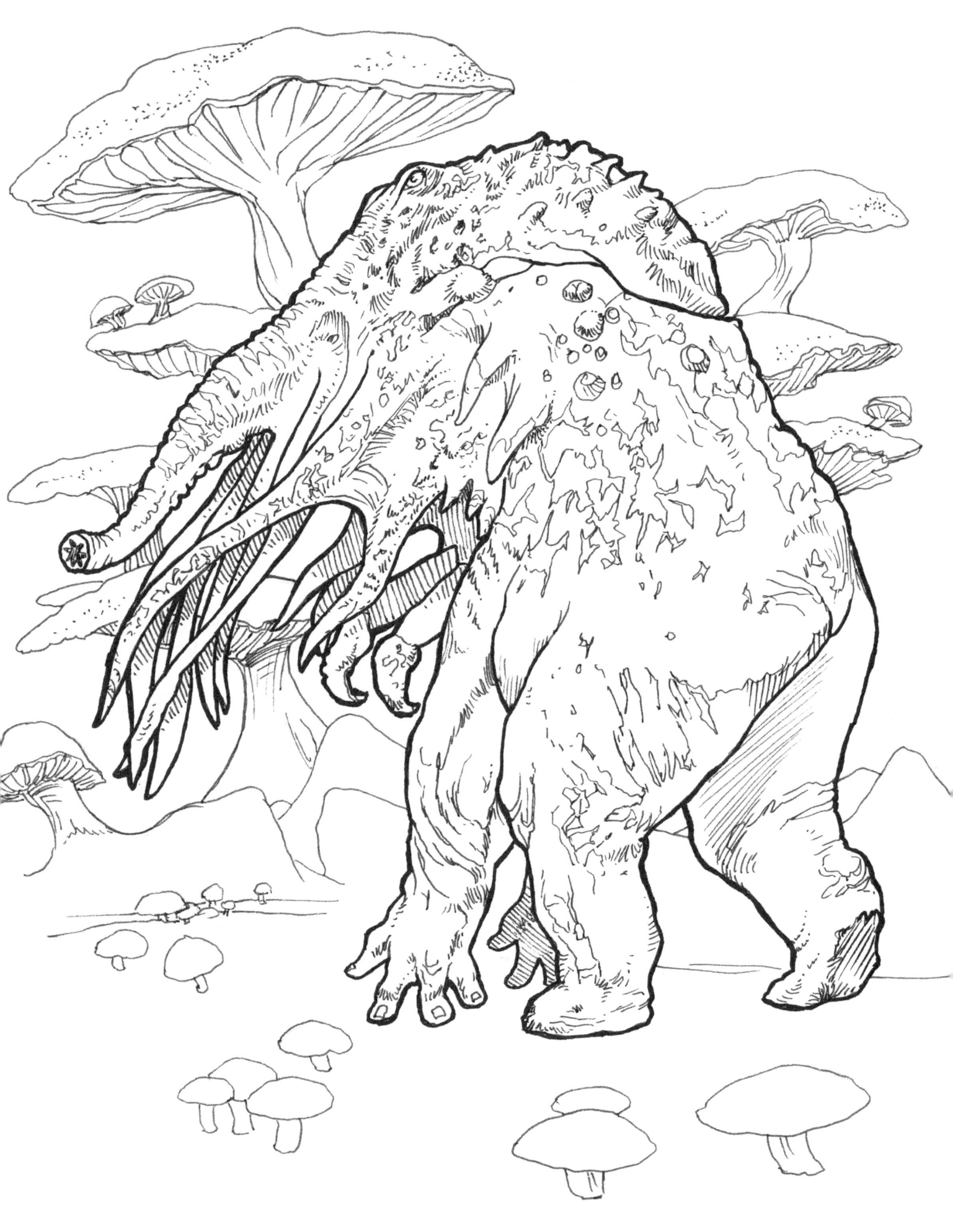

Cthugha

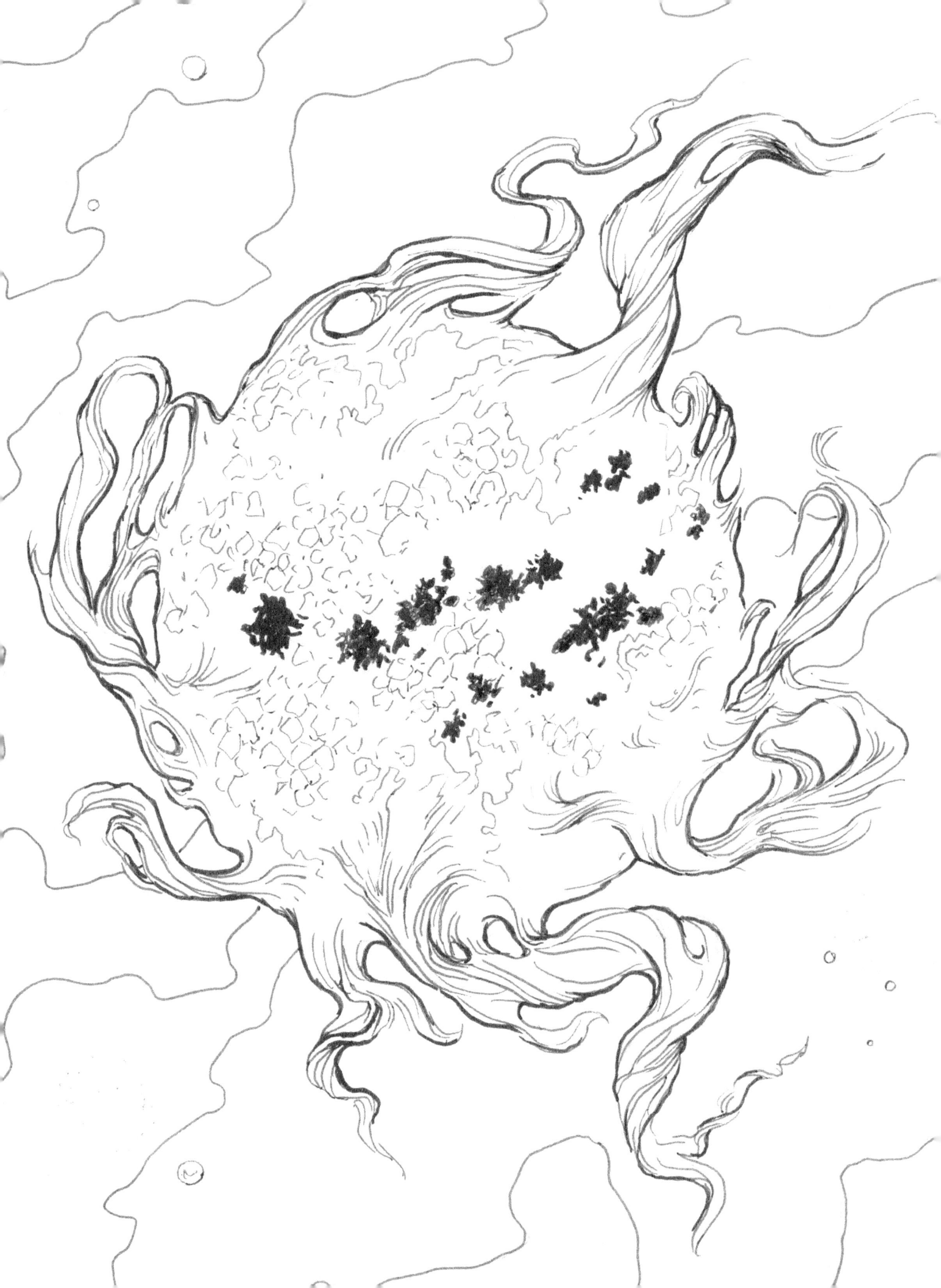

Cthulhu

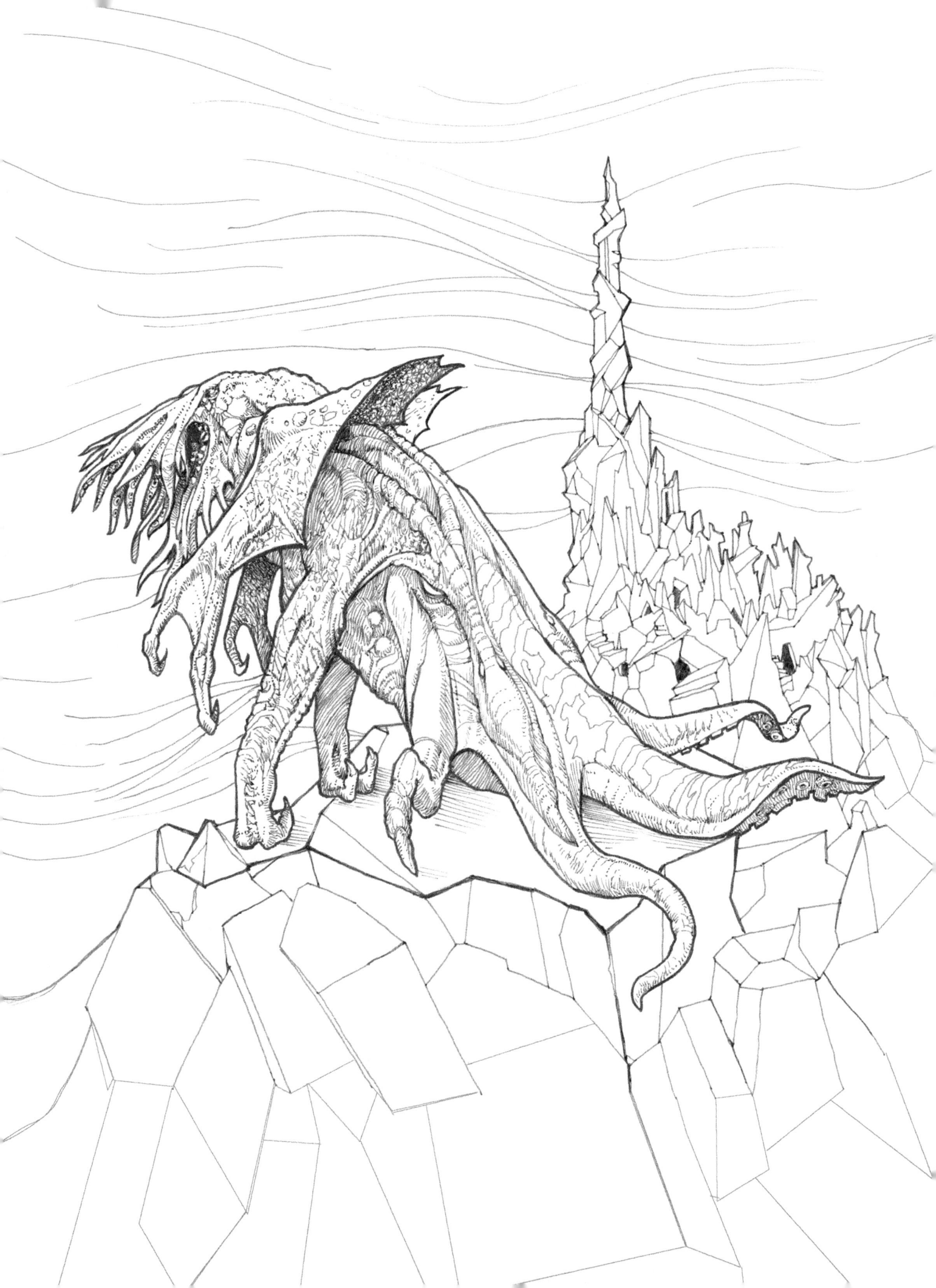

Curwen's Guard

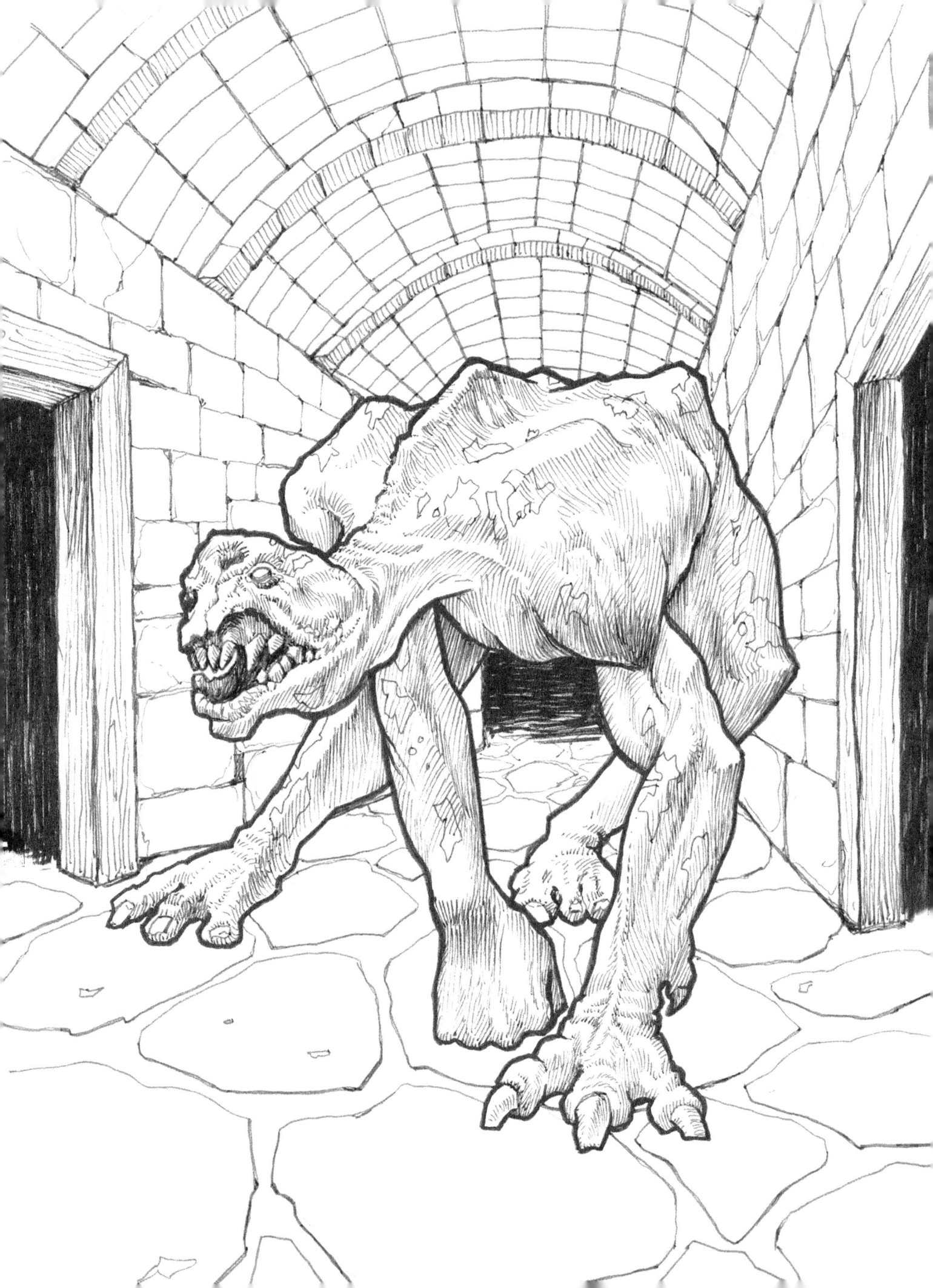

Dagon

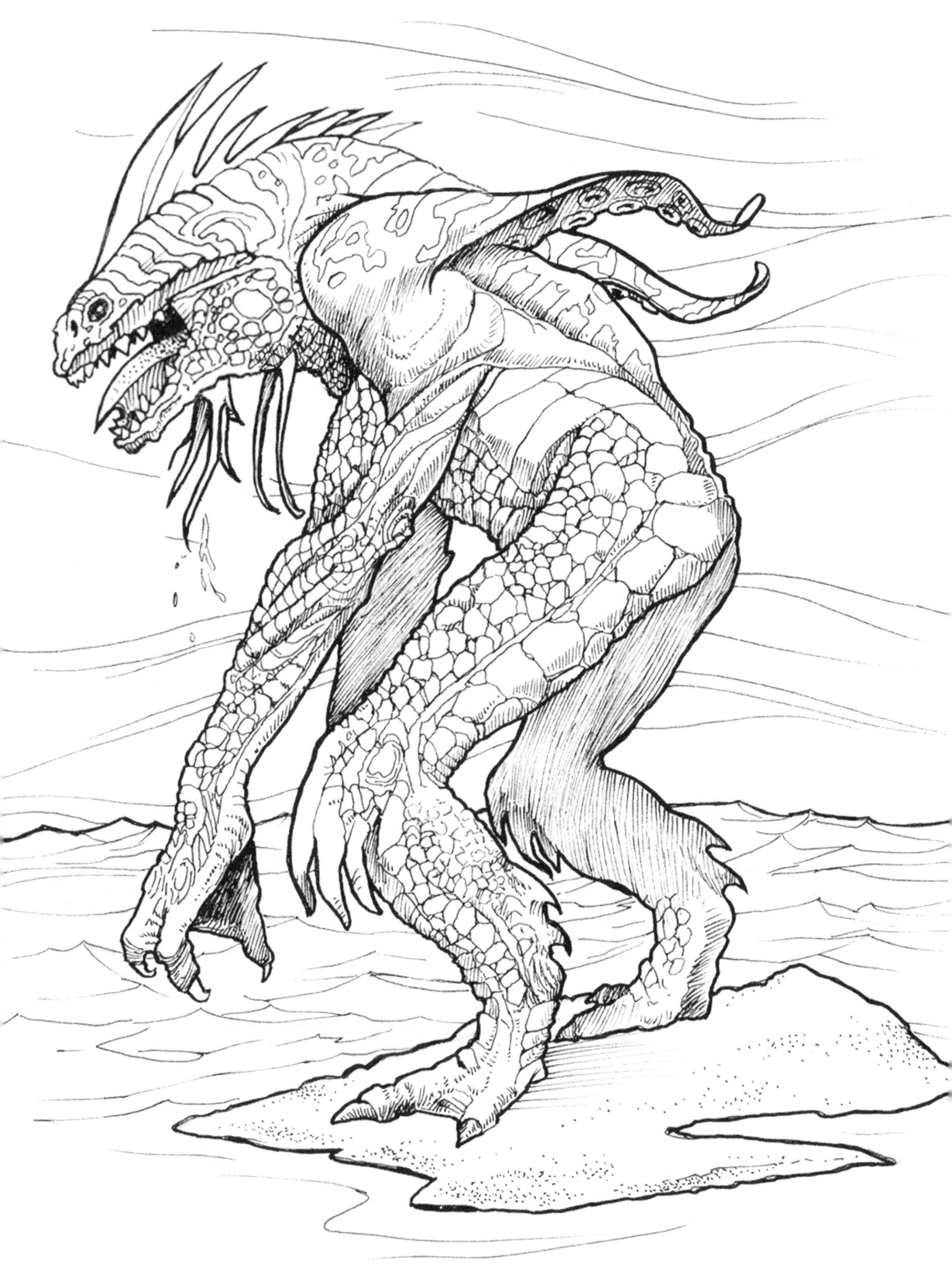

Deep One

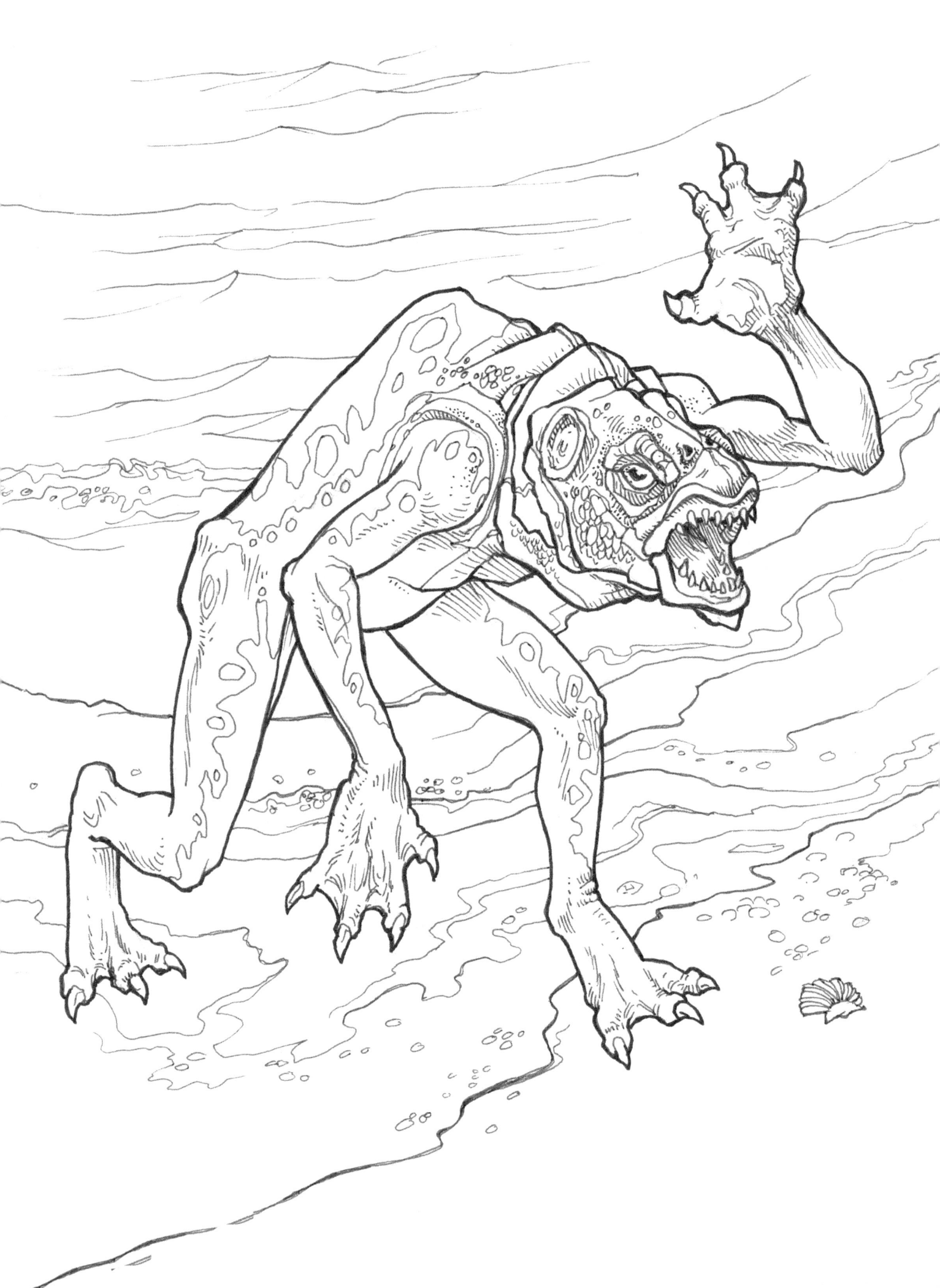

Dhole

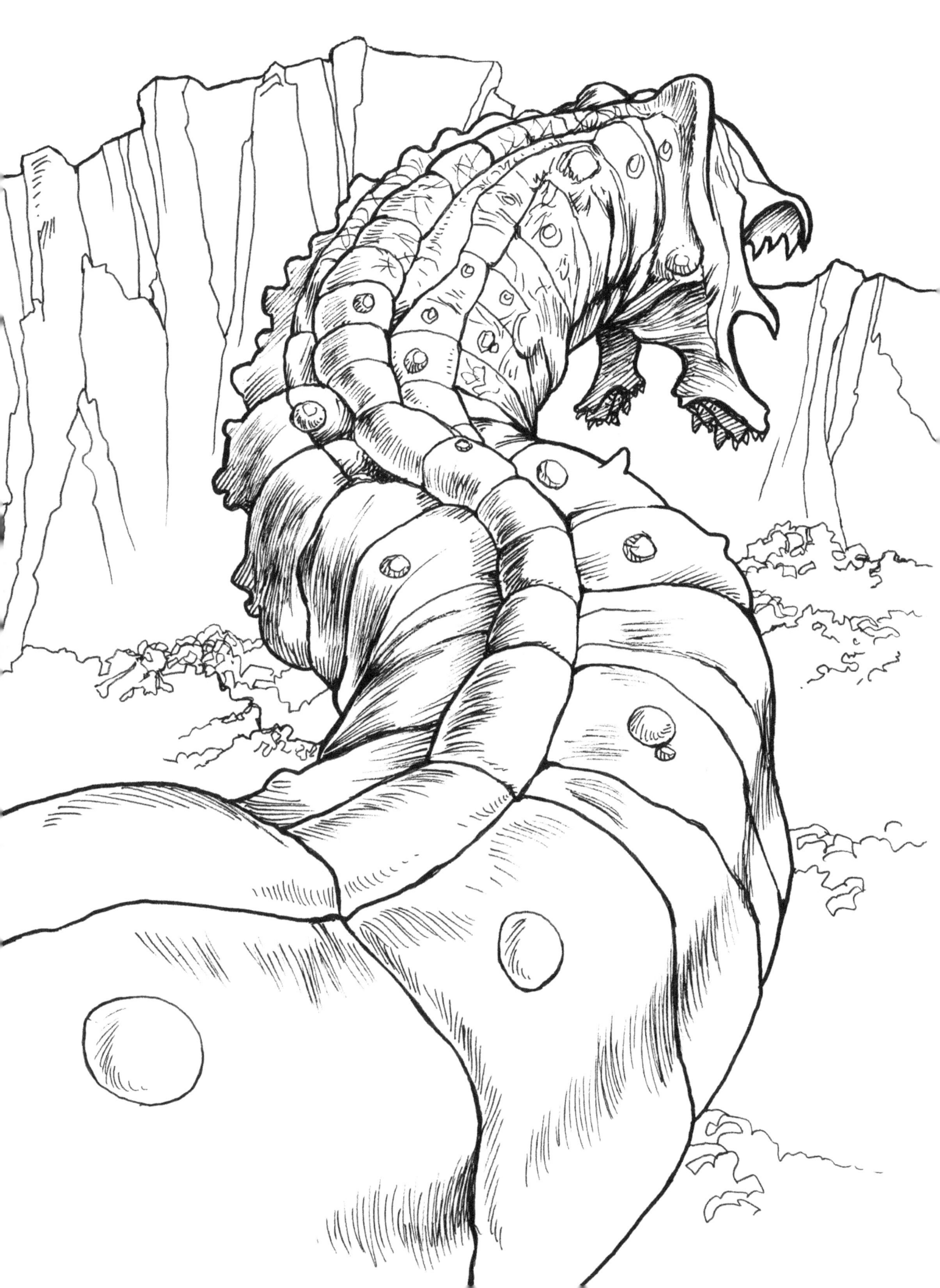

Elder Thing

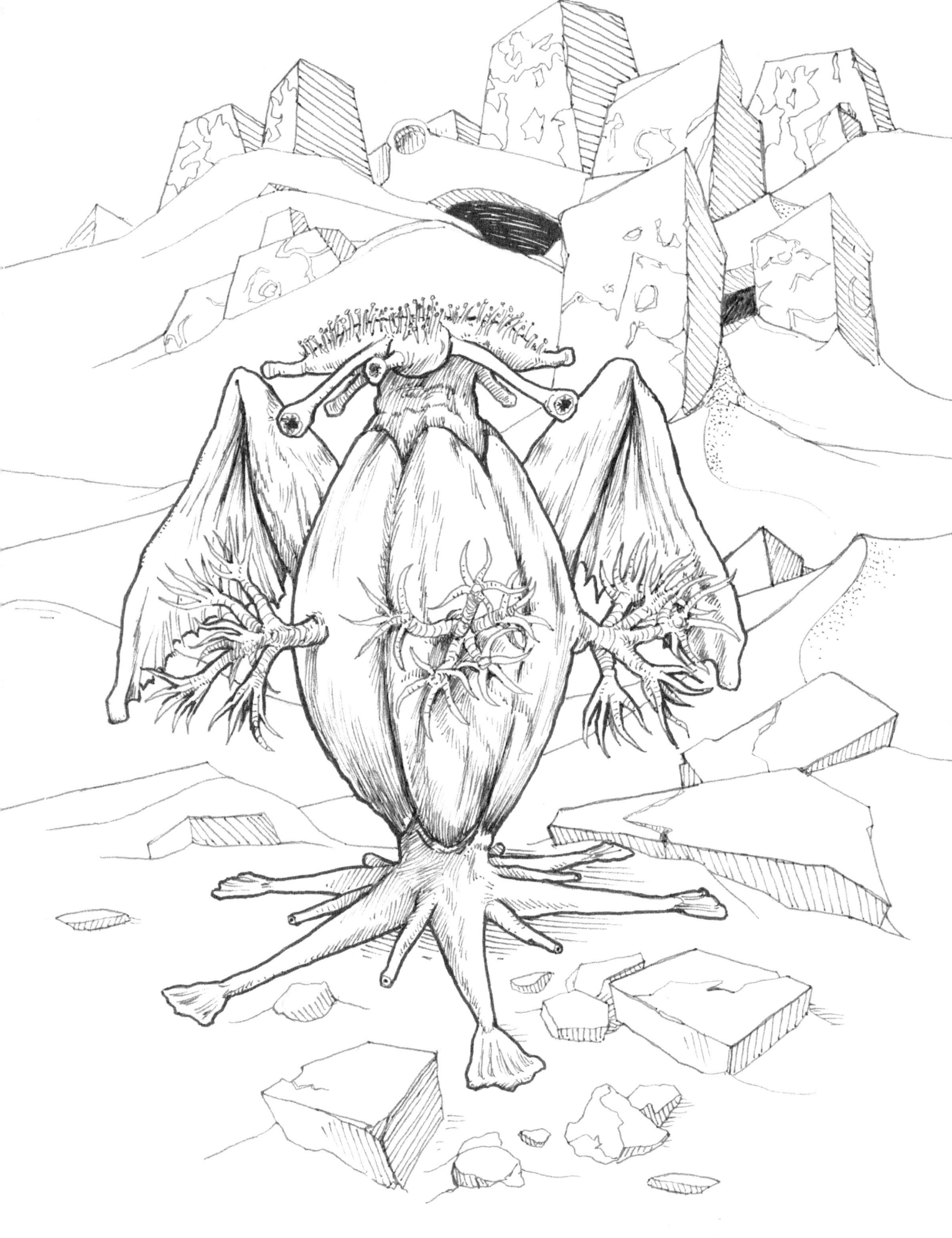

Ghast

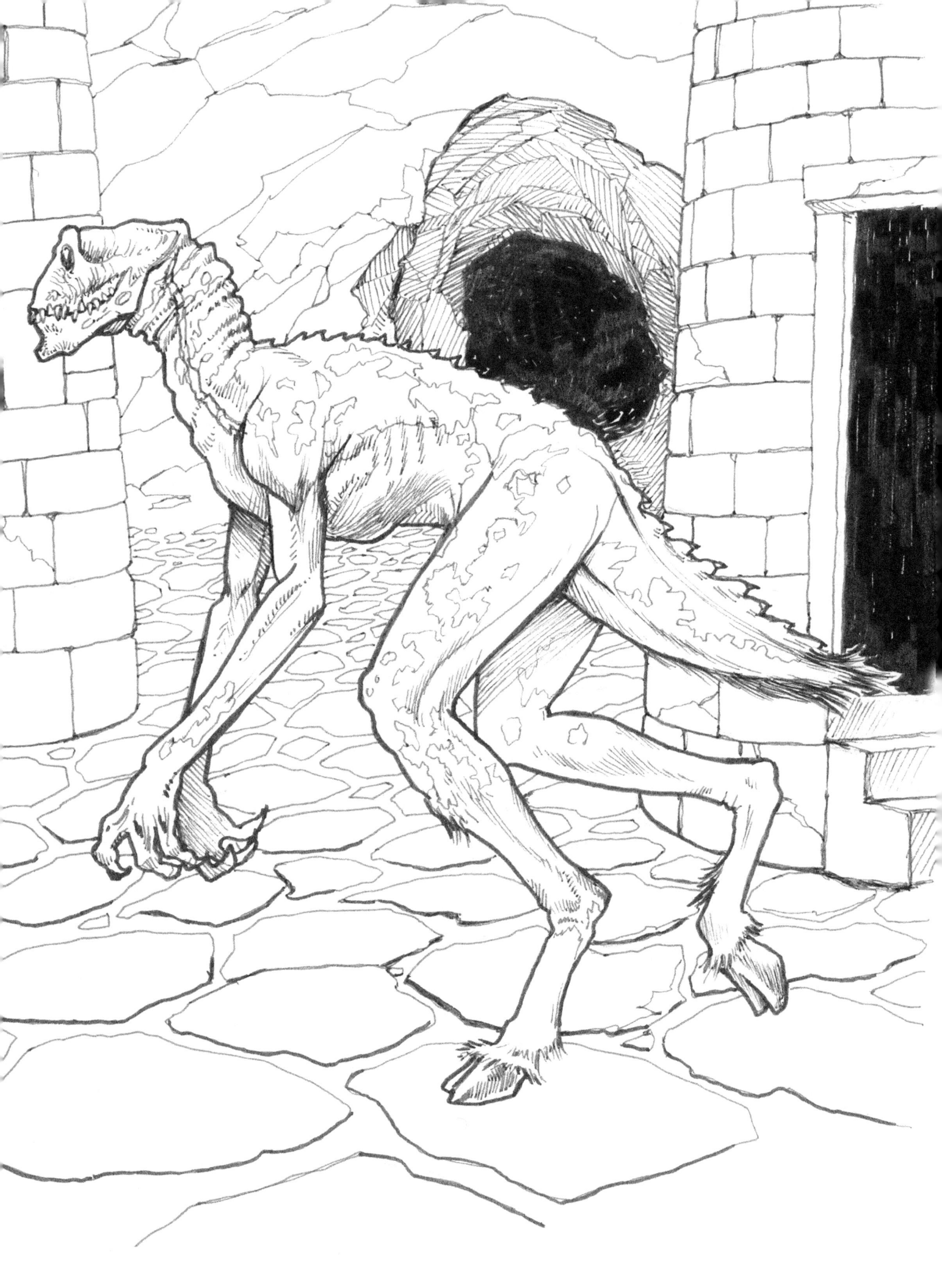

Ghatanothoa

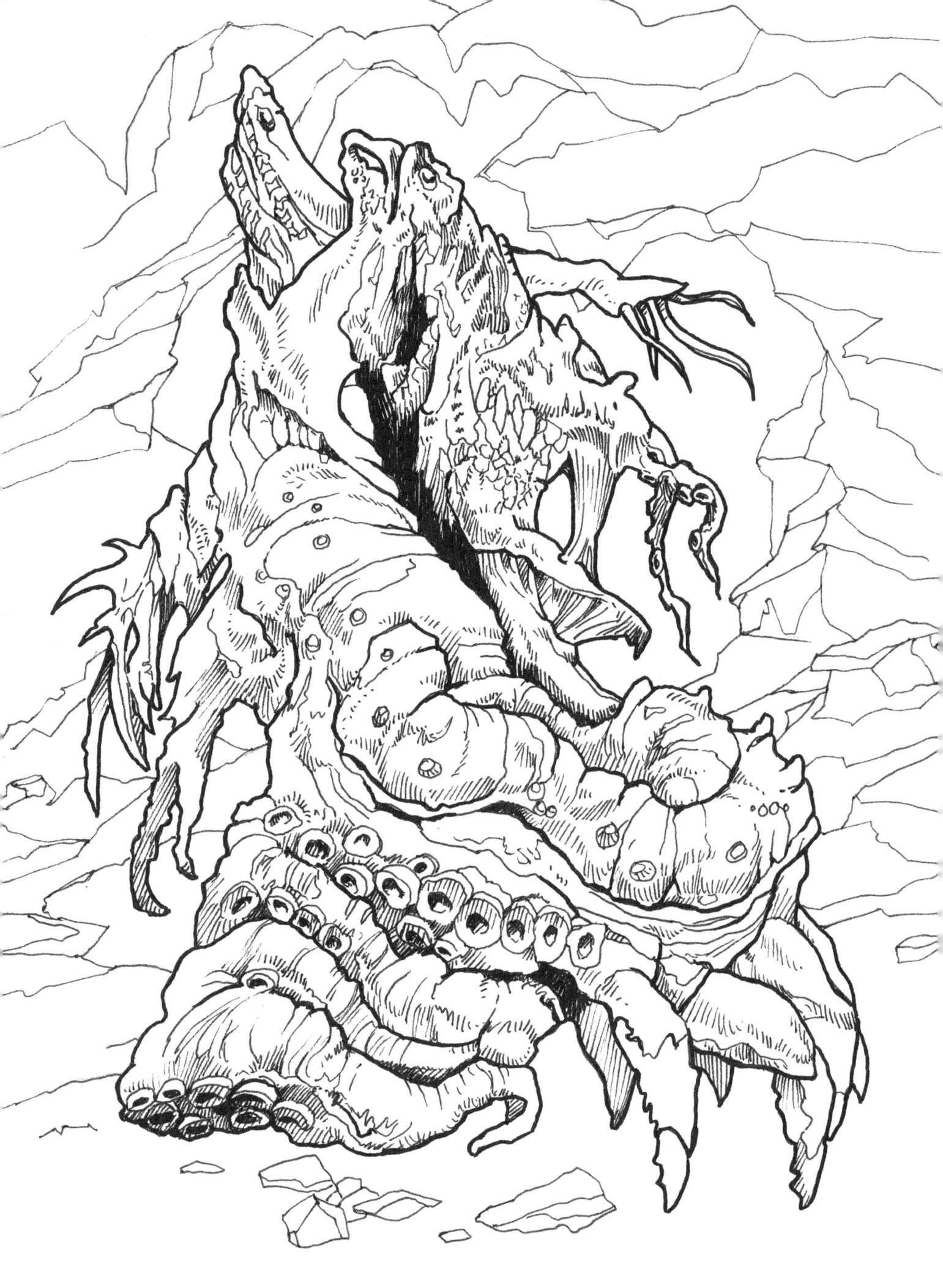

Ghoul

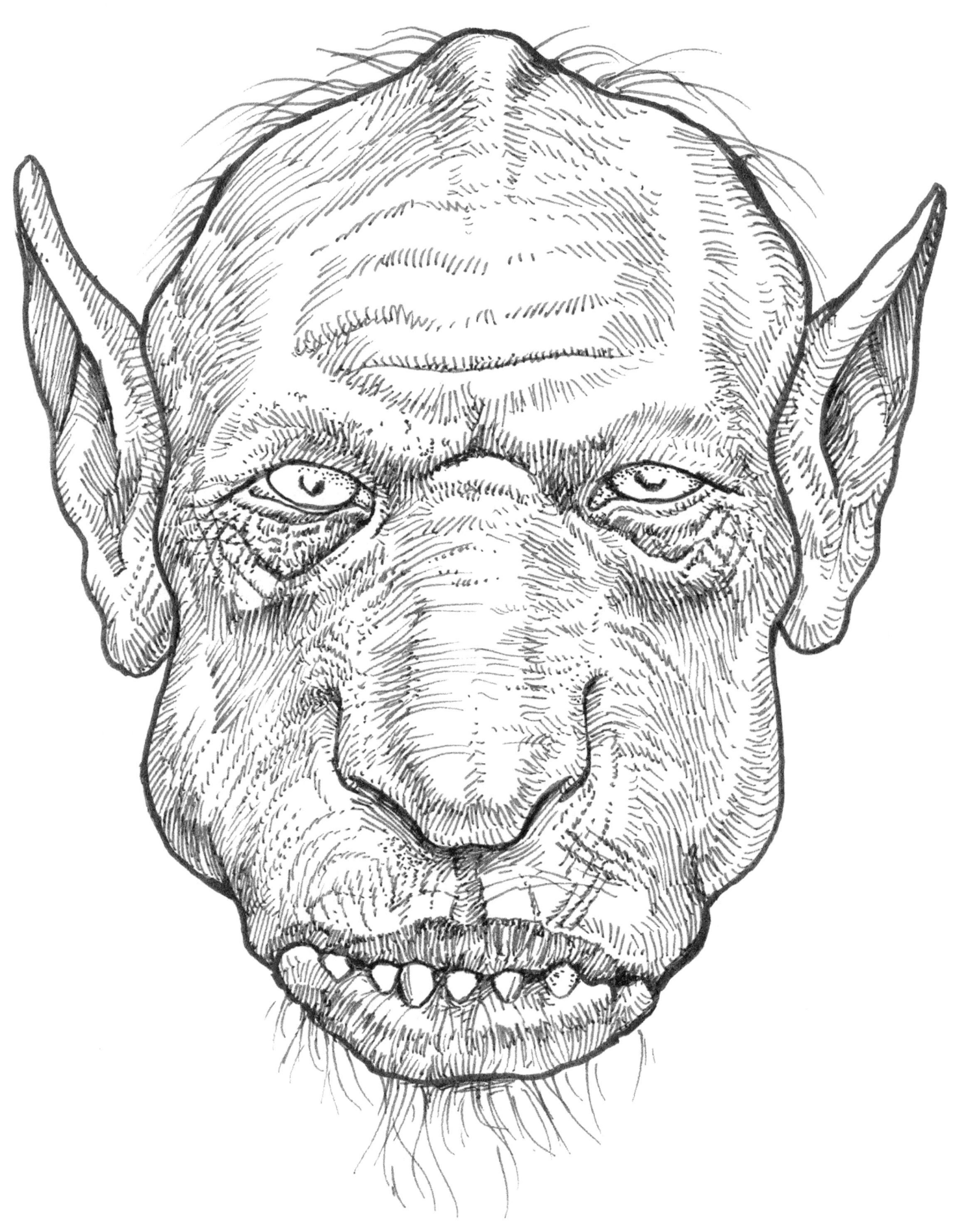

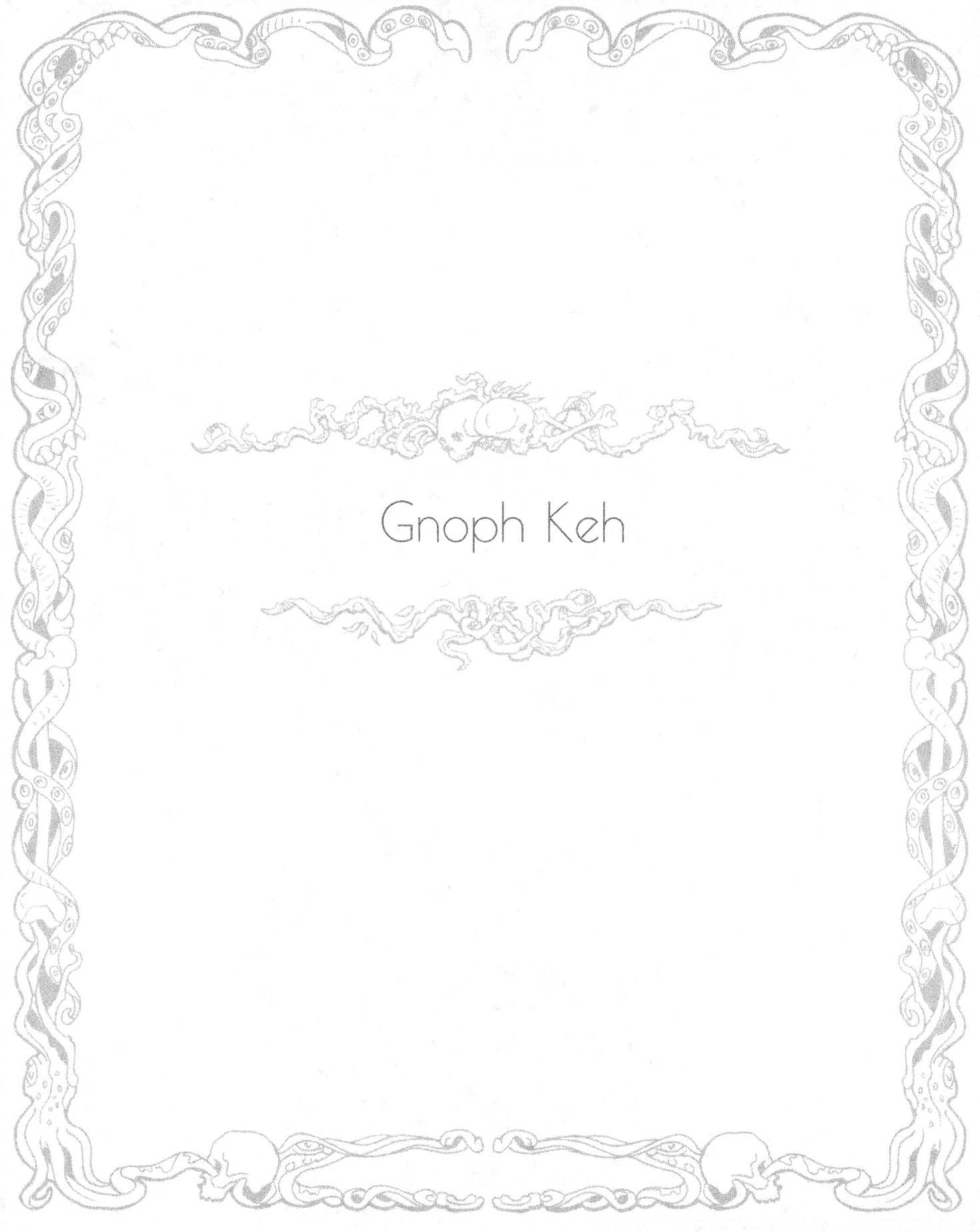

Gnoph Keh

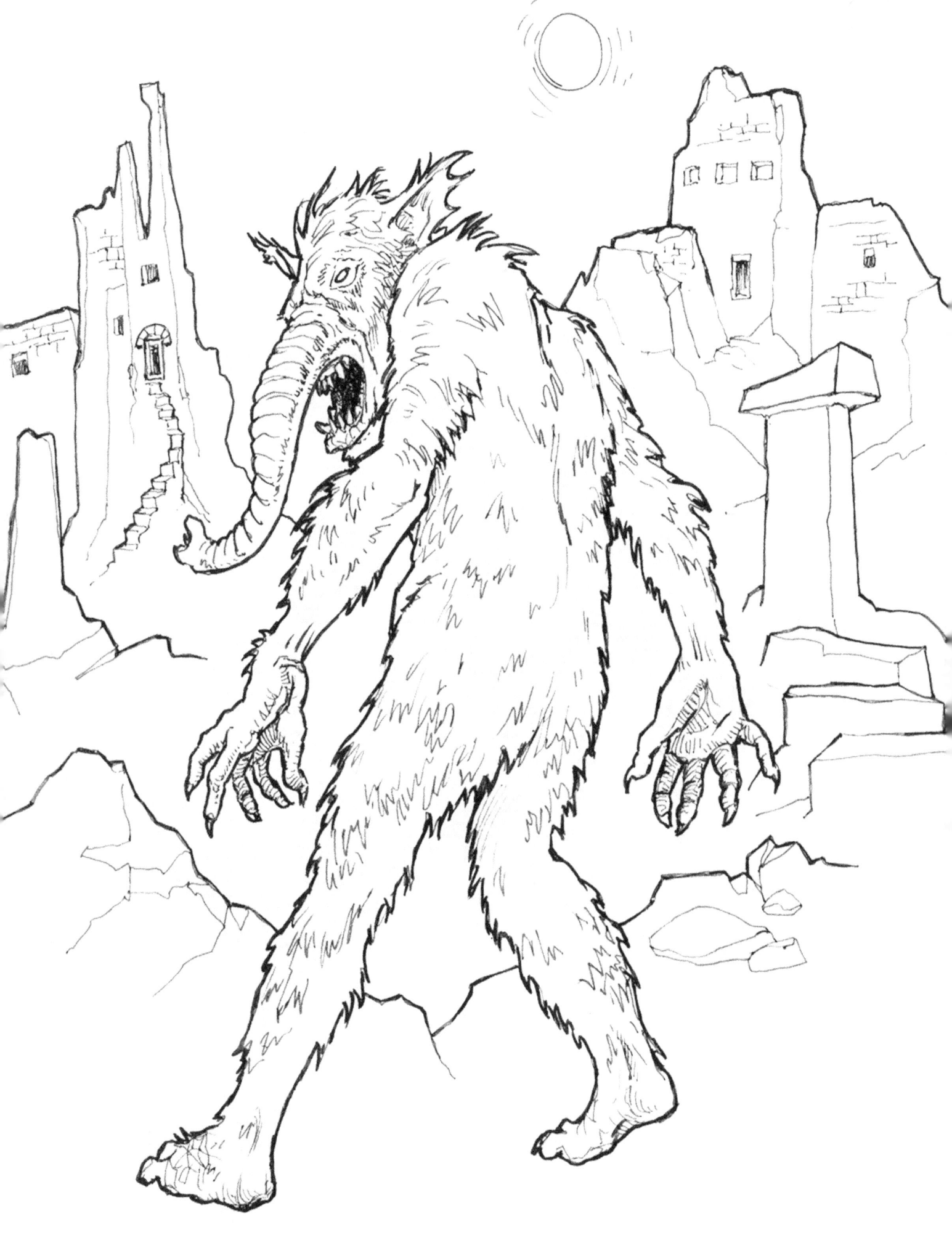

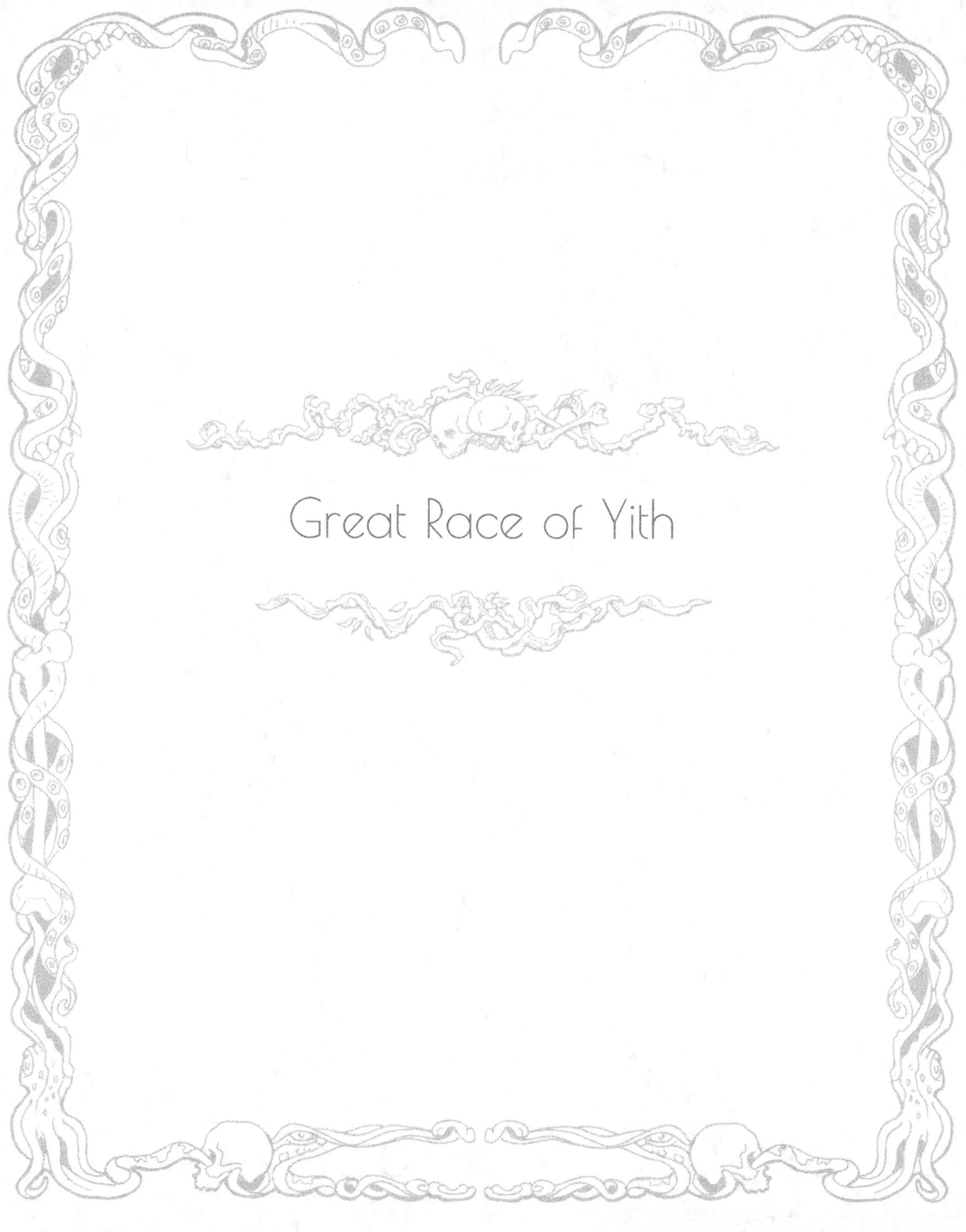

Great Race of Yith

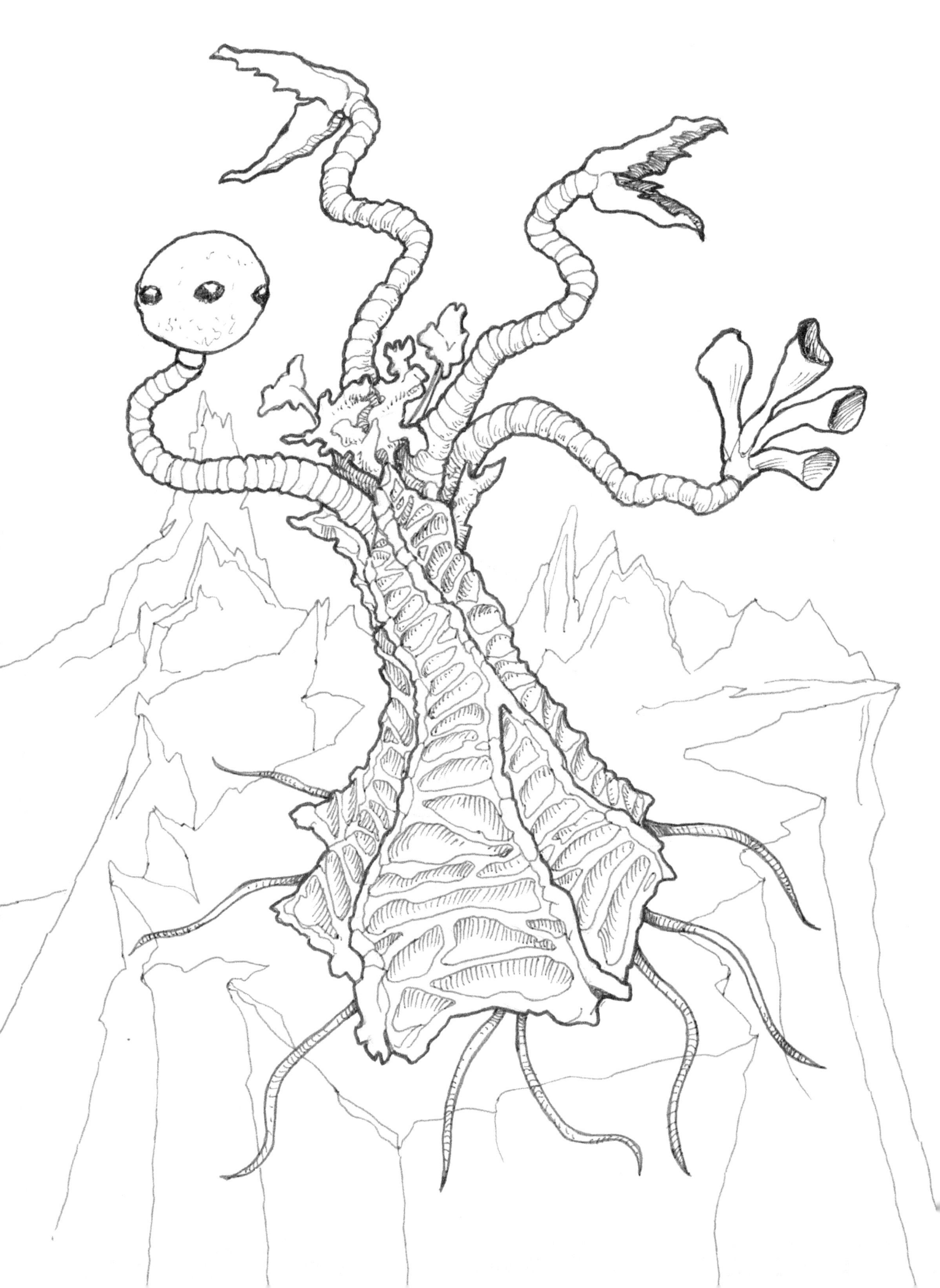

Hastur

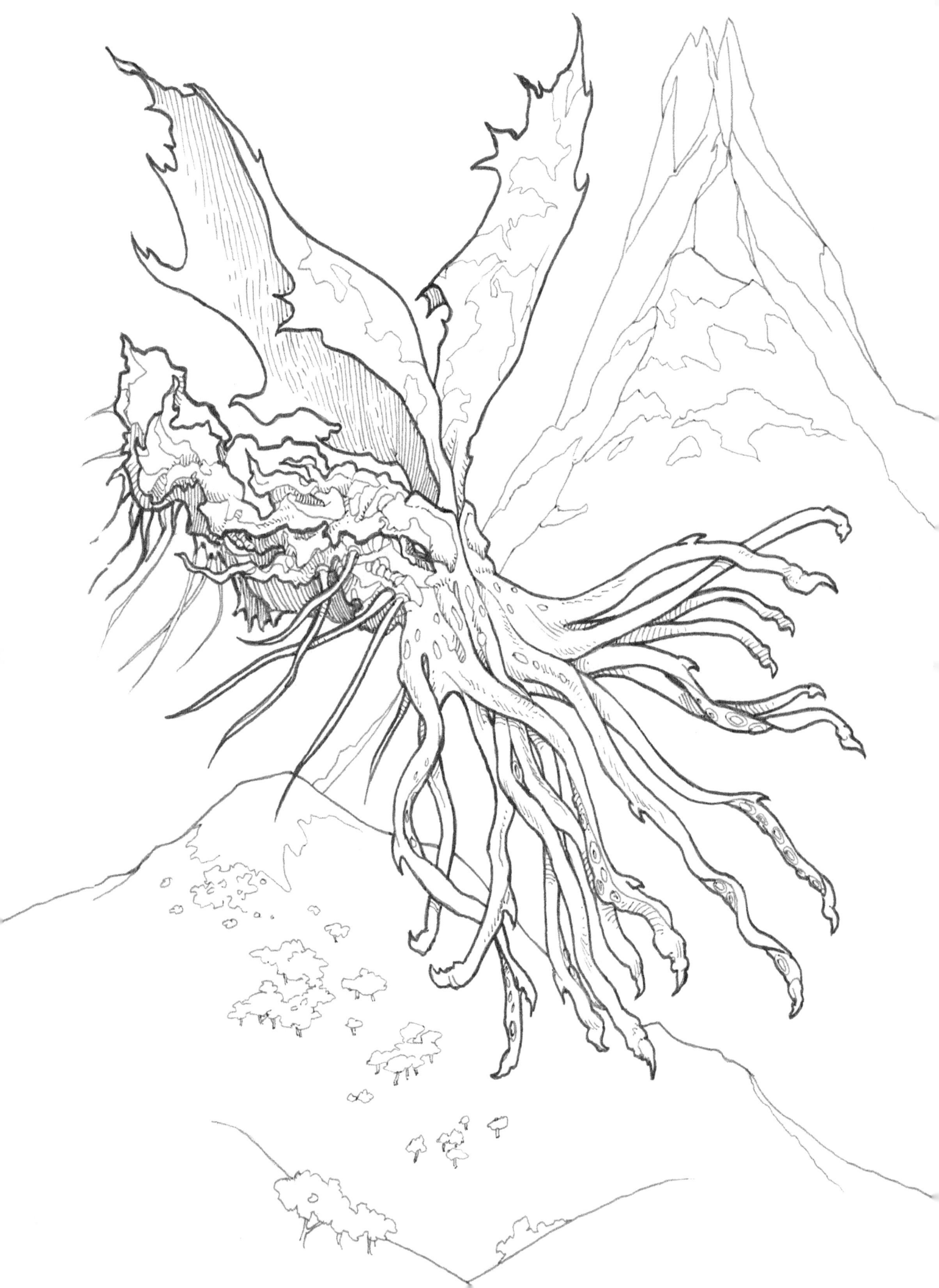

Ithaqua

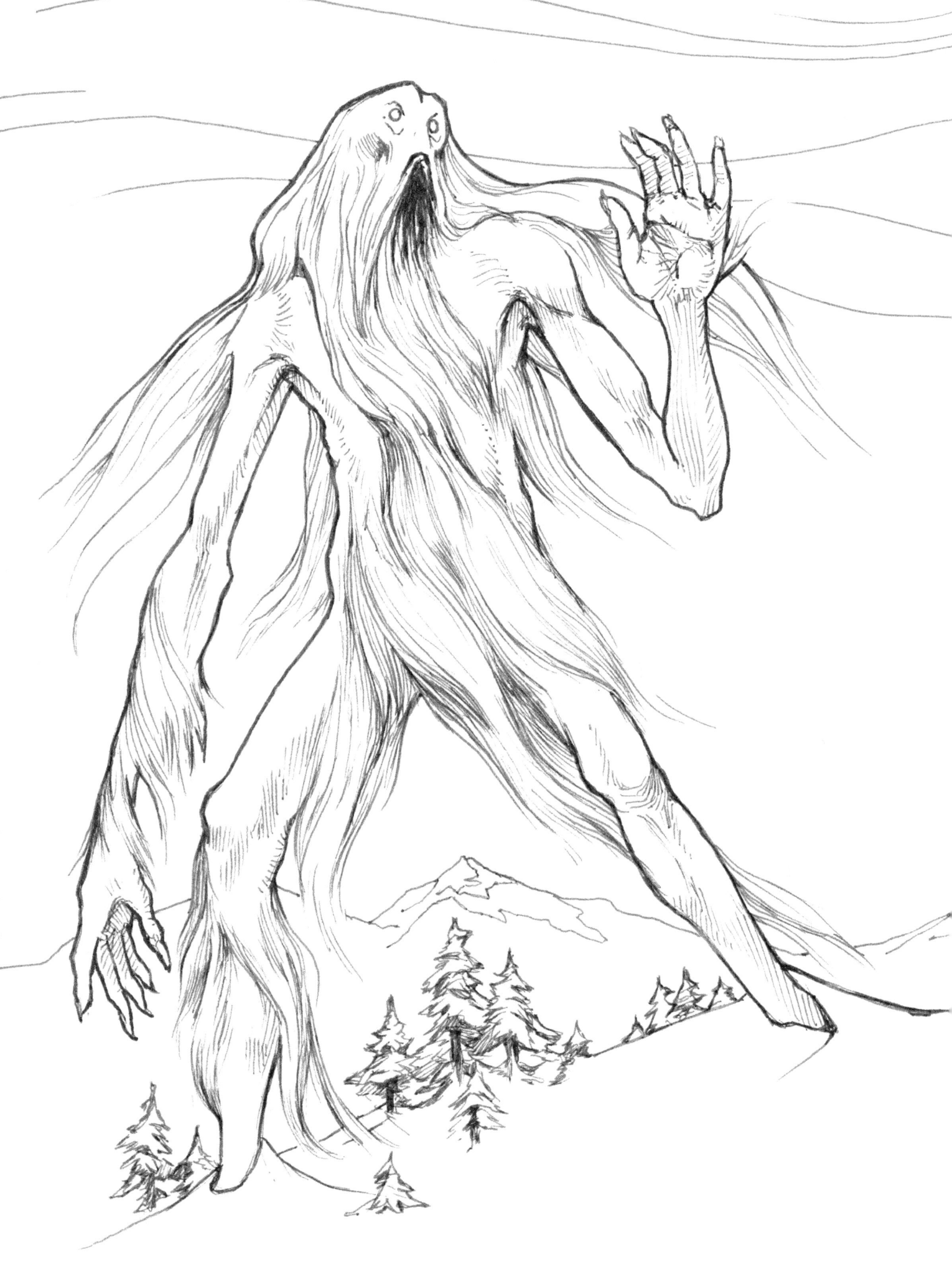

Larva of the Elder Gods

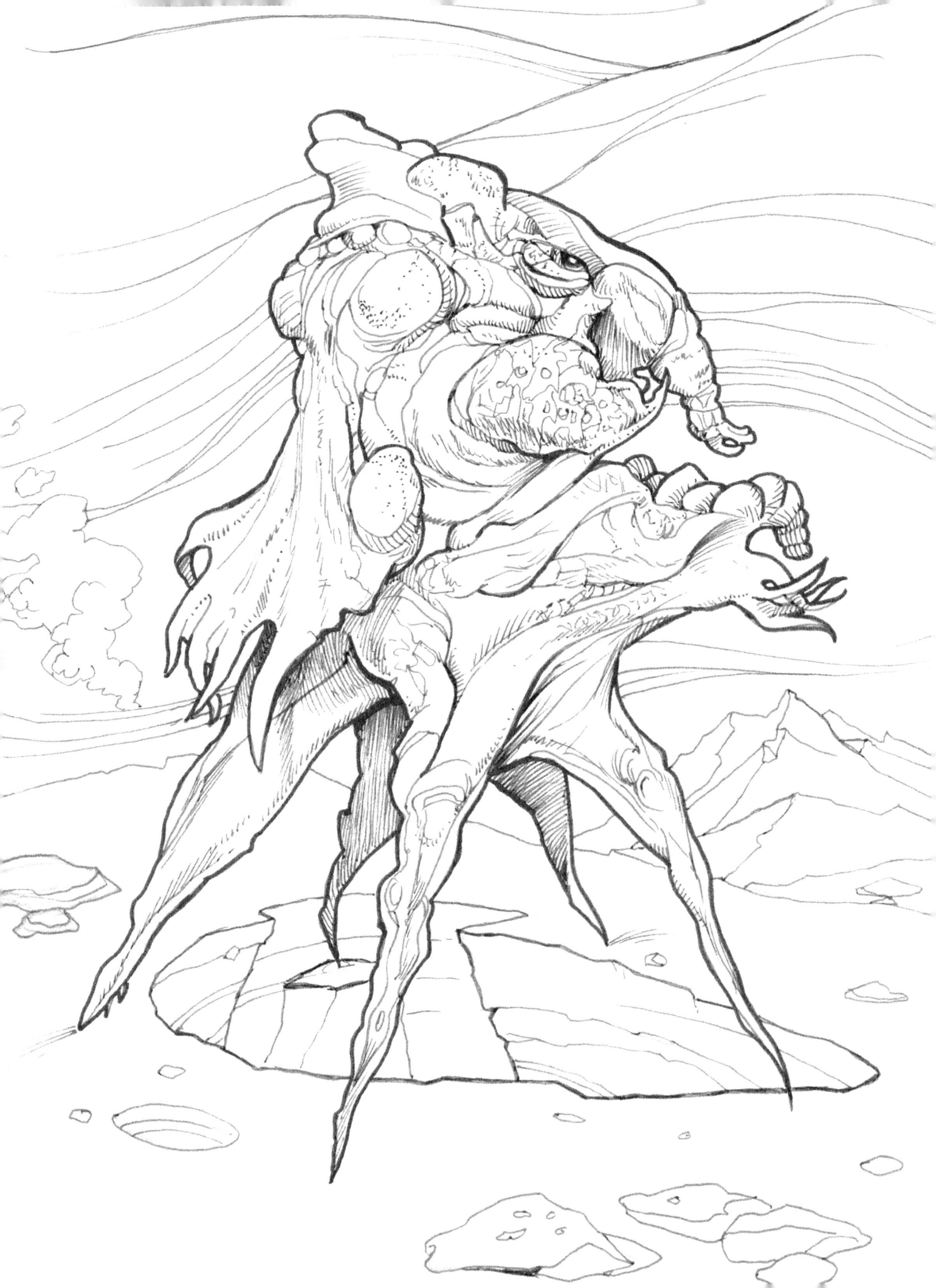

Mi-Go

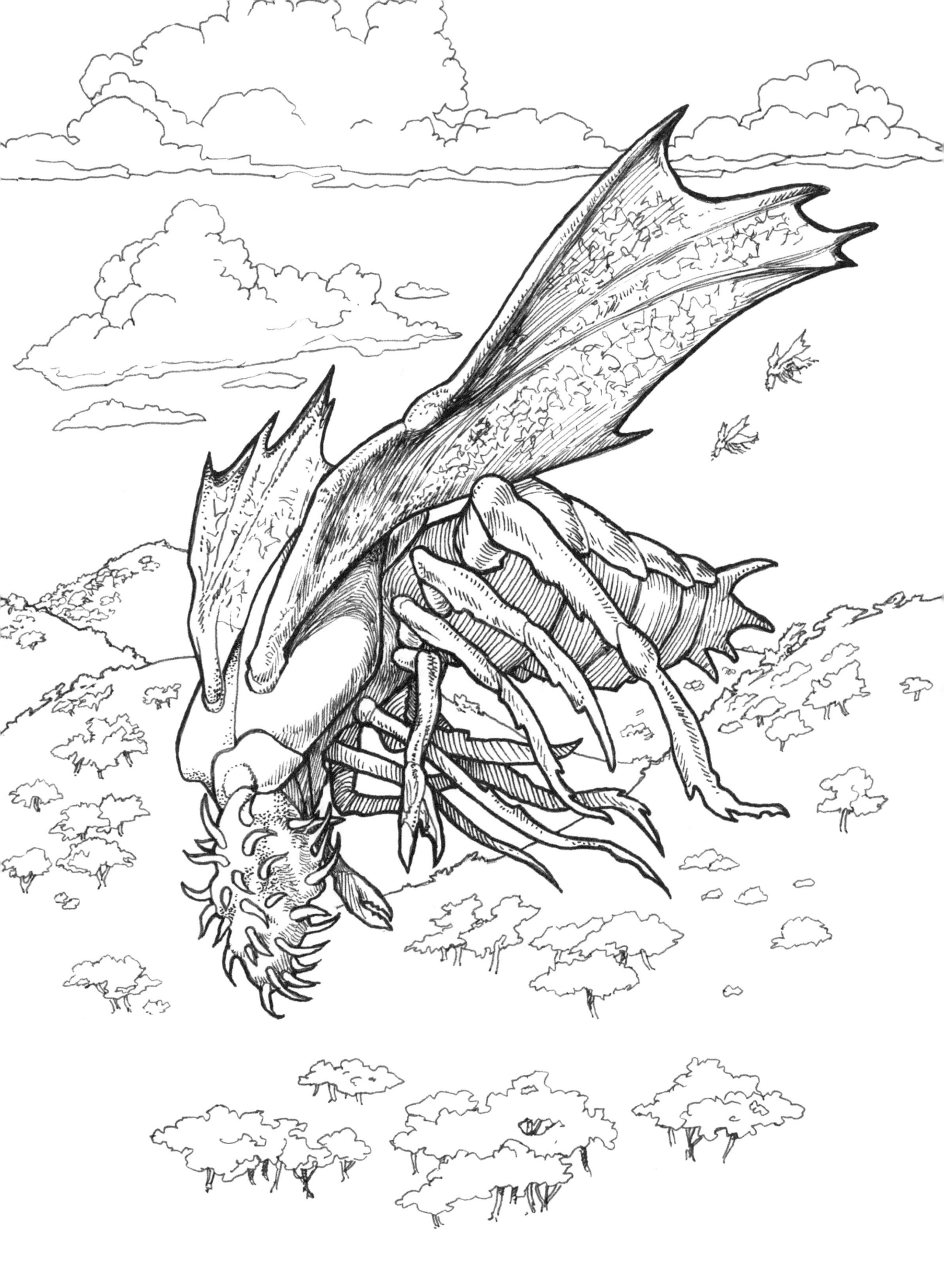

Night Gaunt

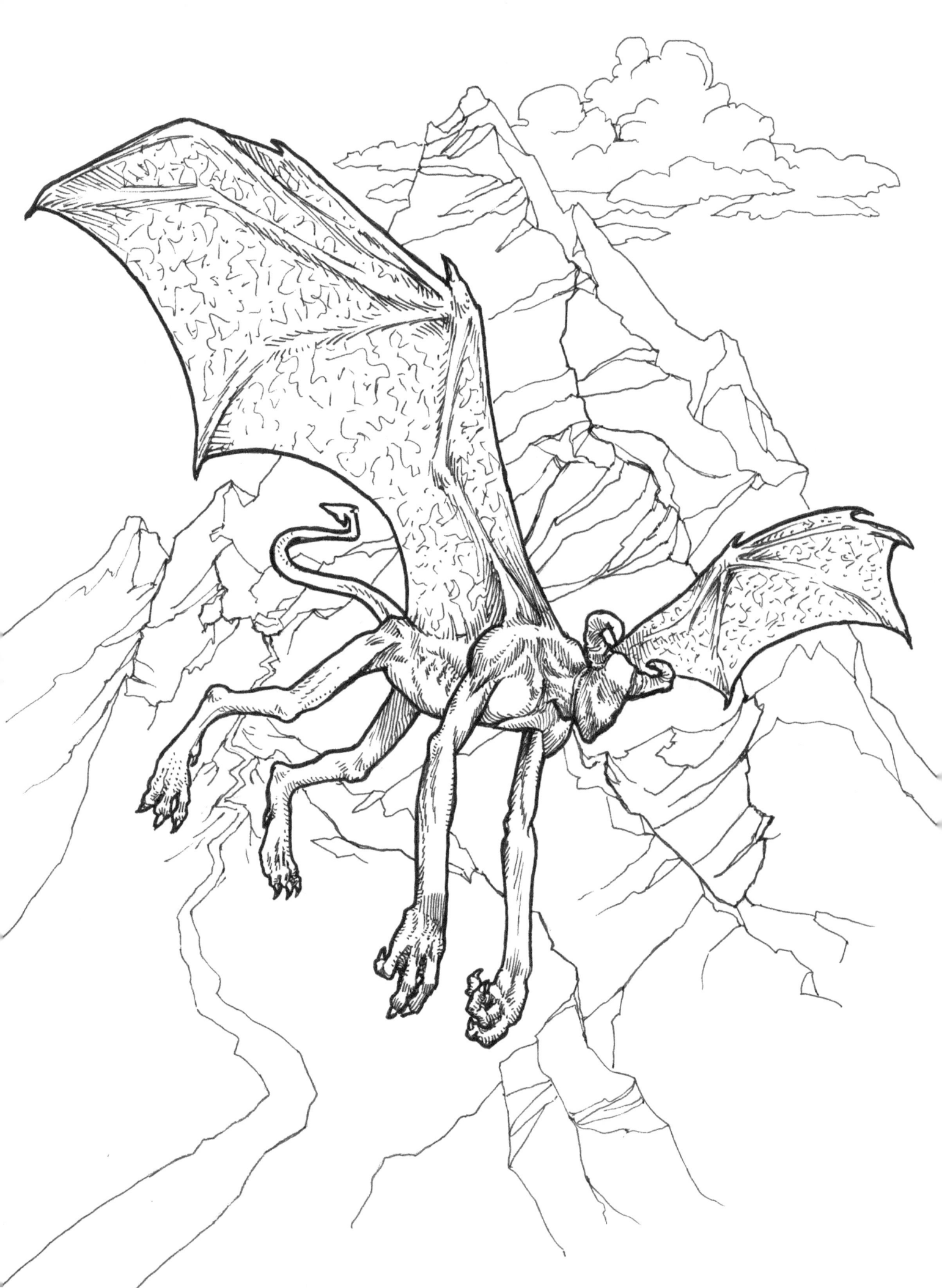

Nyarlathotep

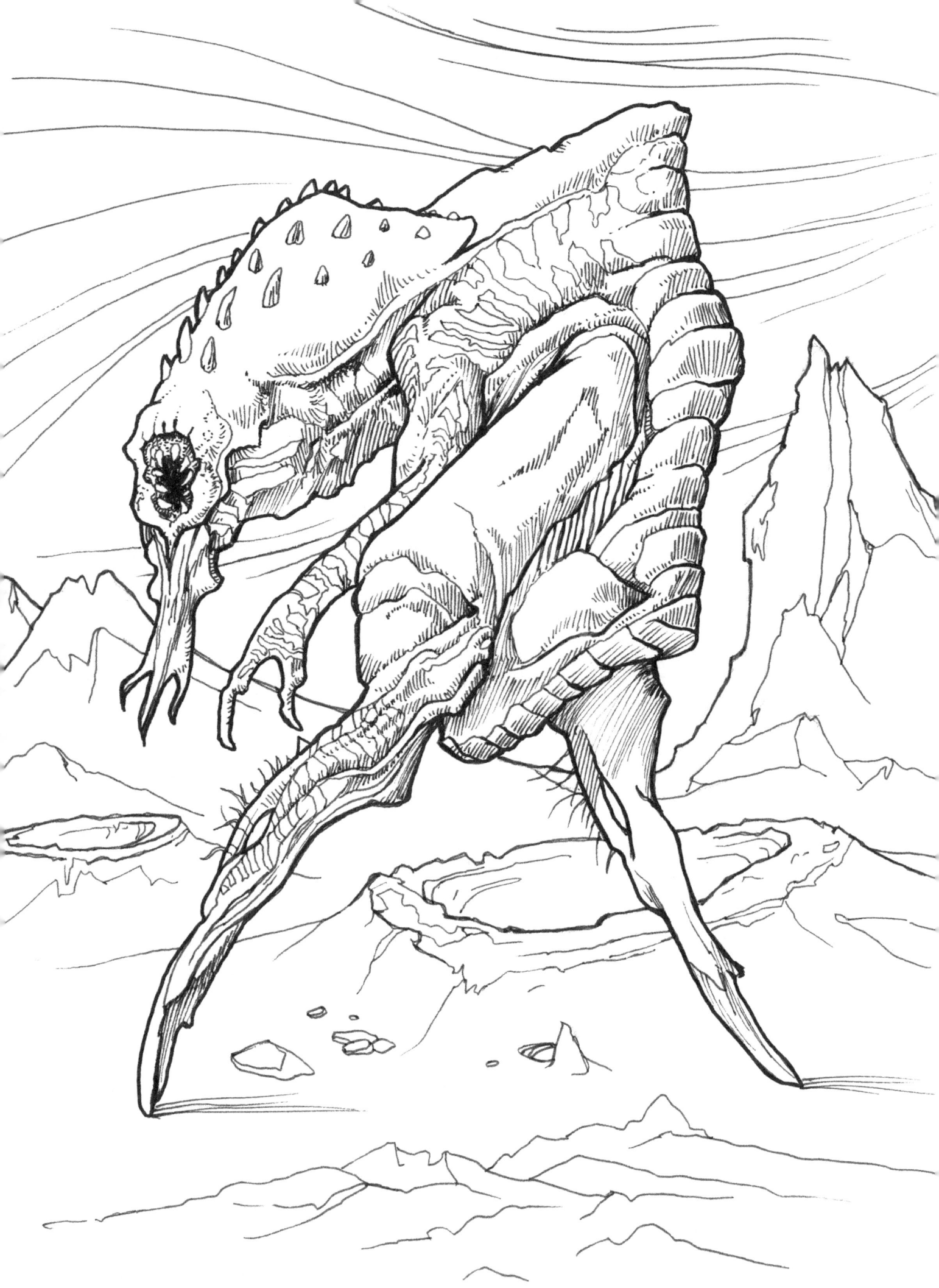

Other God

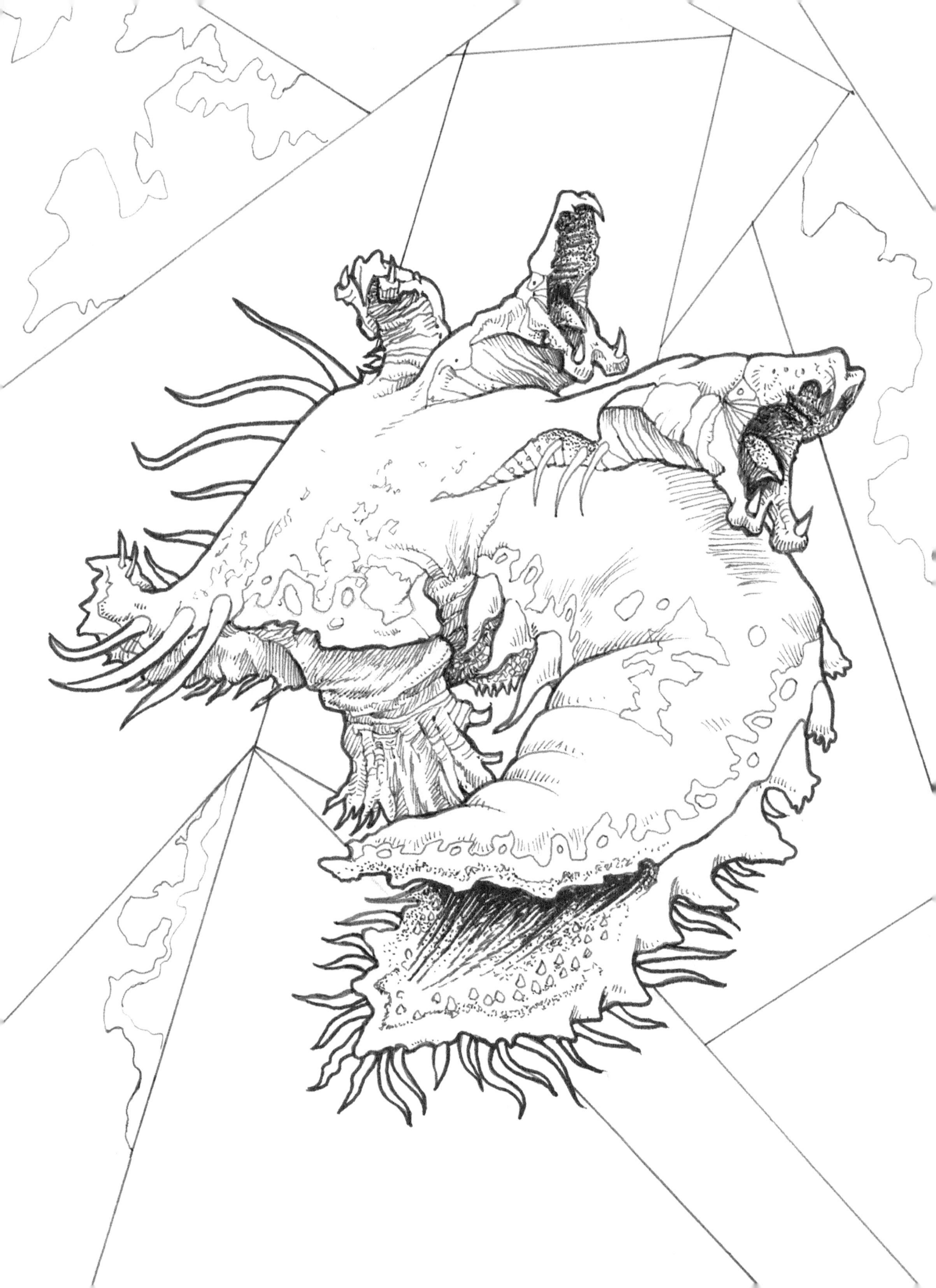

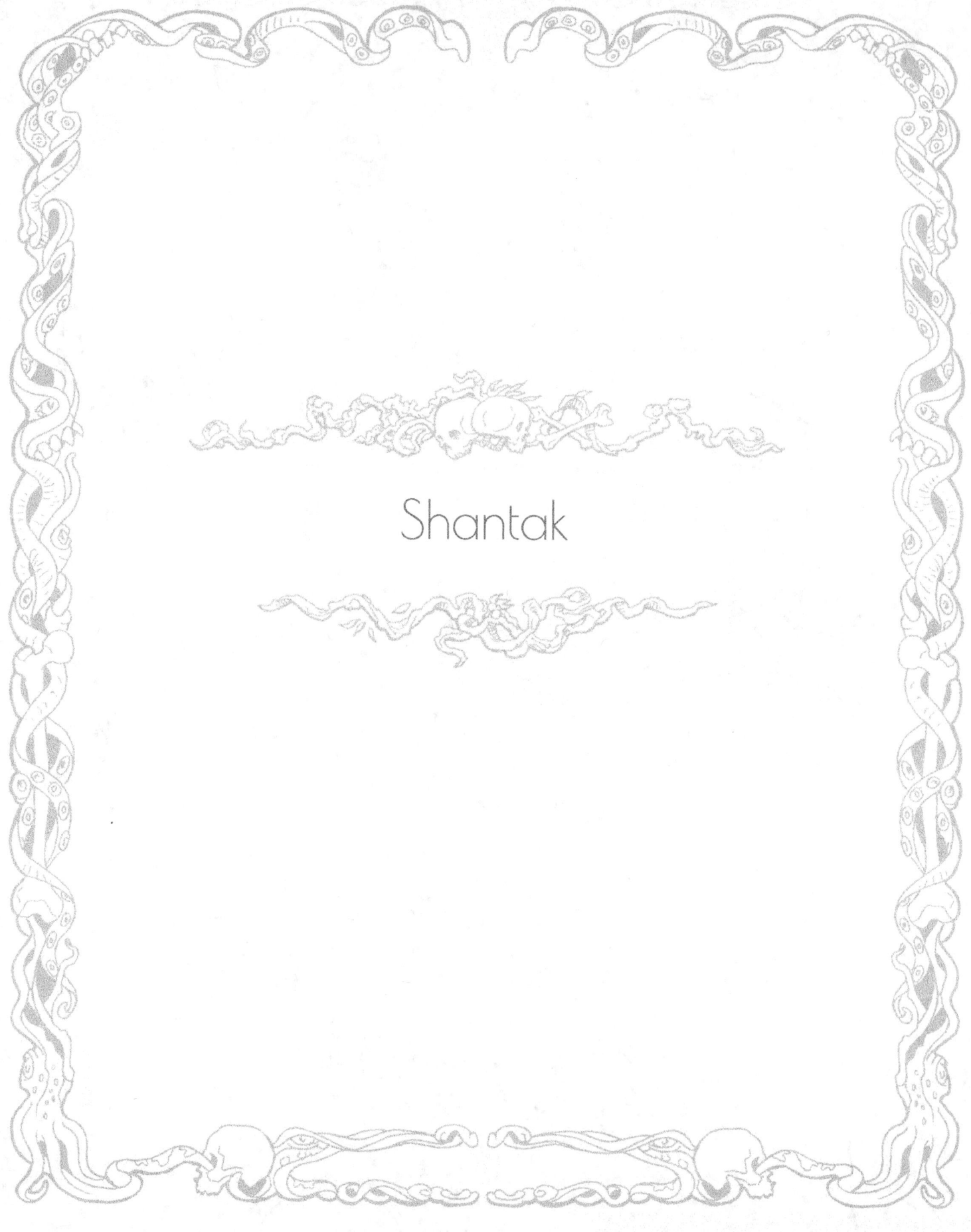

Shantak

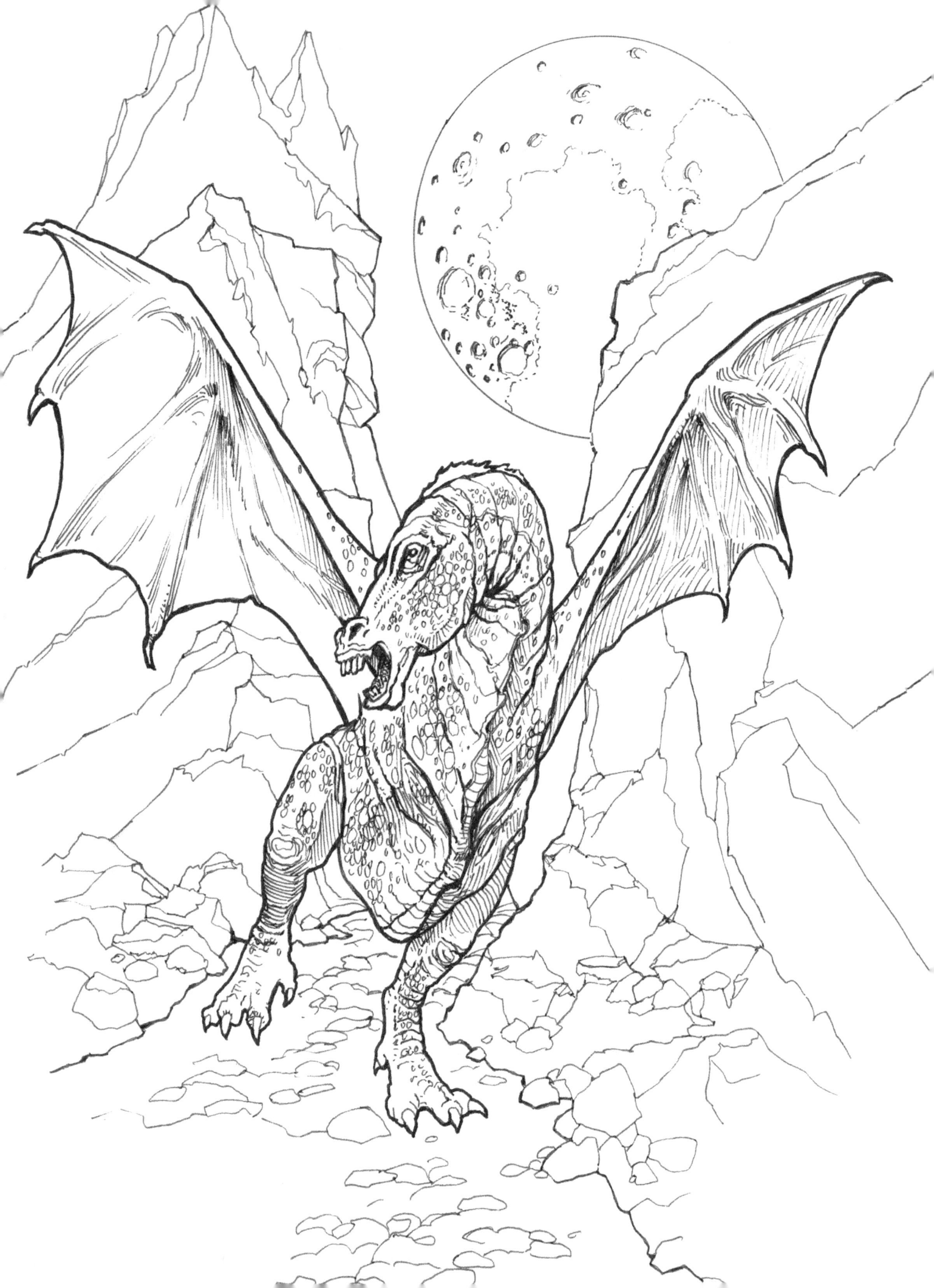

Shoggoth

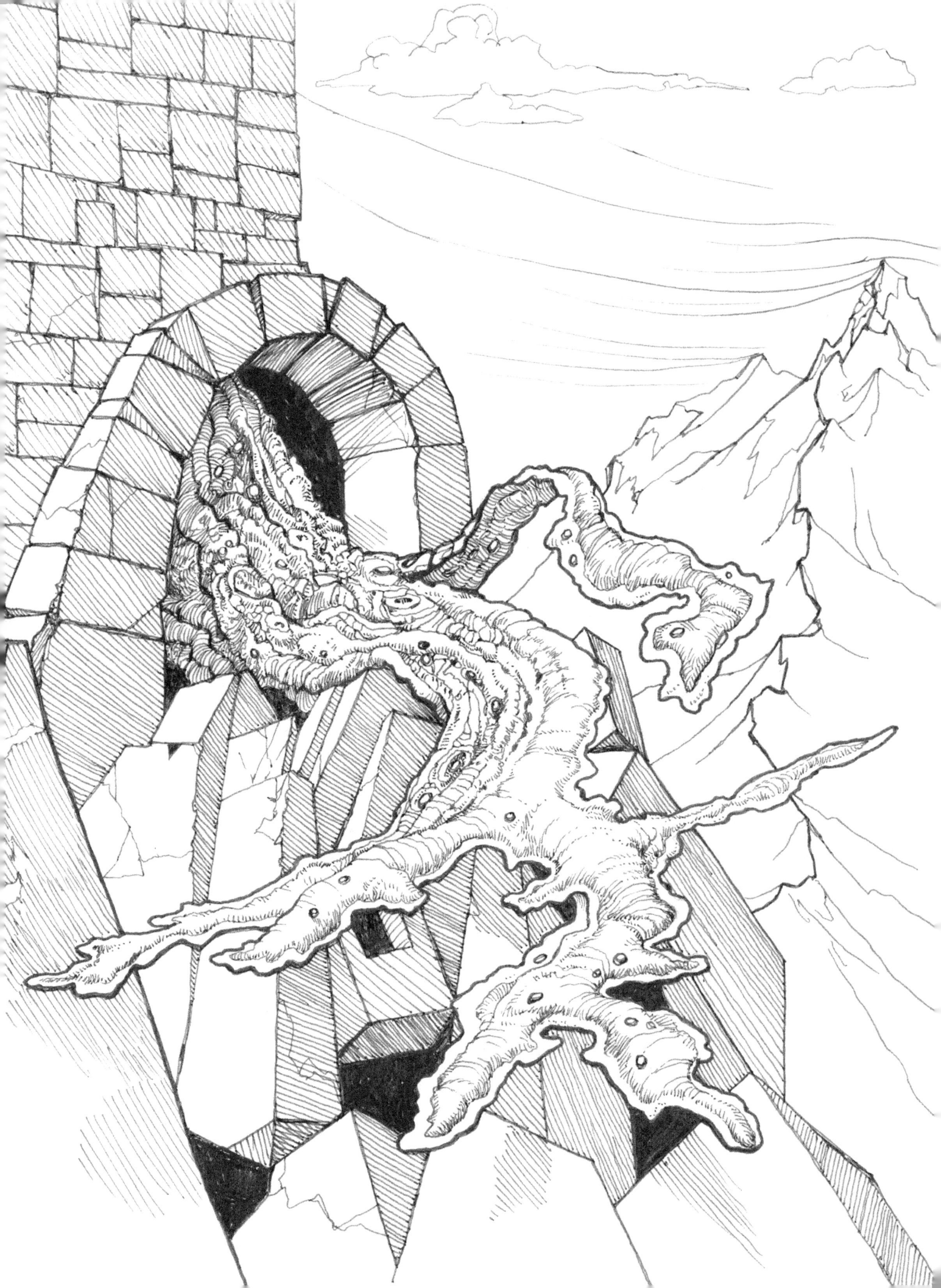

Shub-Niggurath

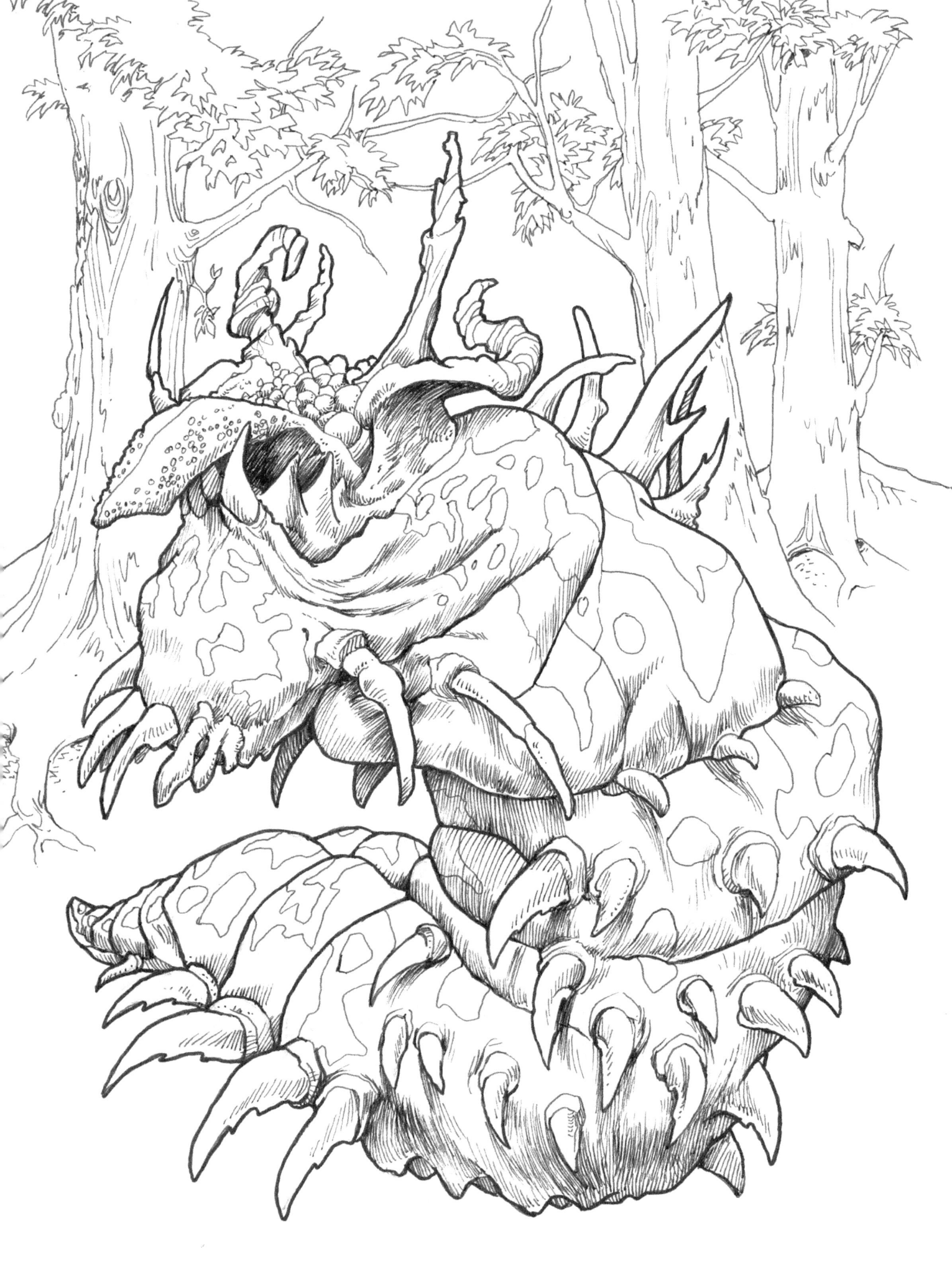

Tsathoggua

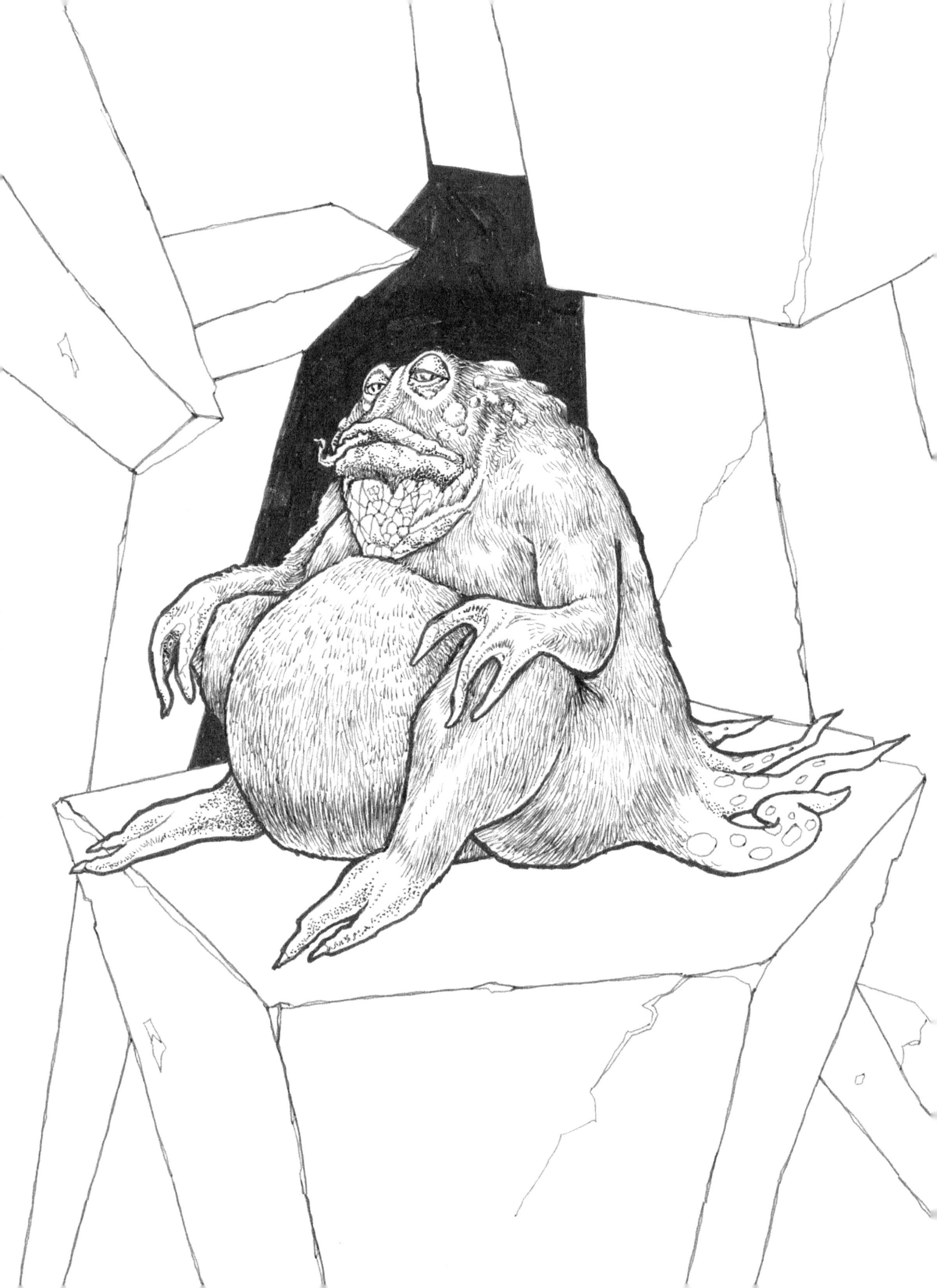

Yeb

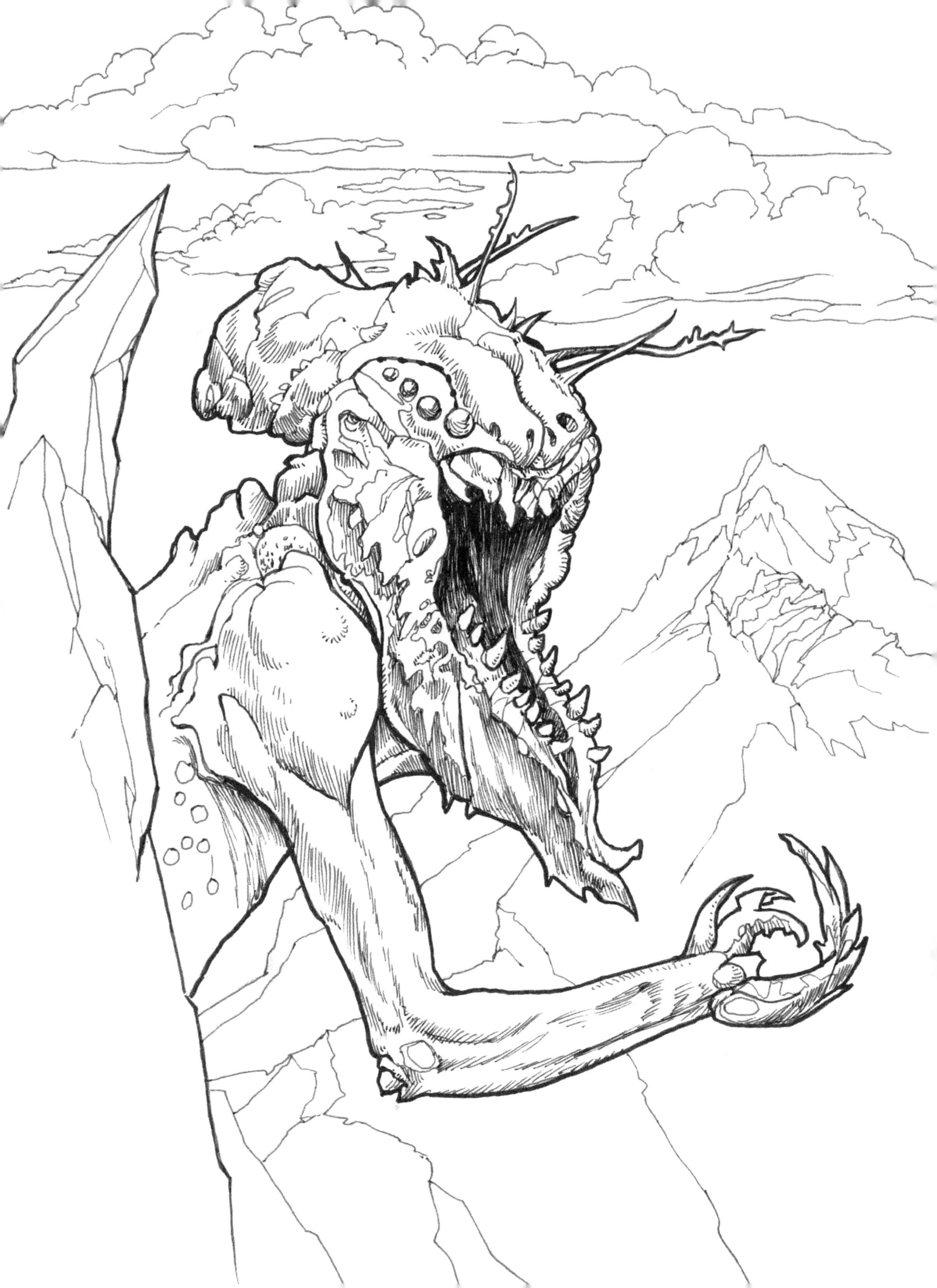

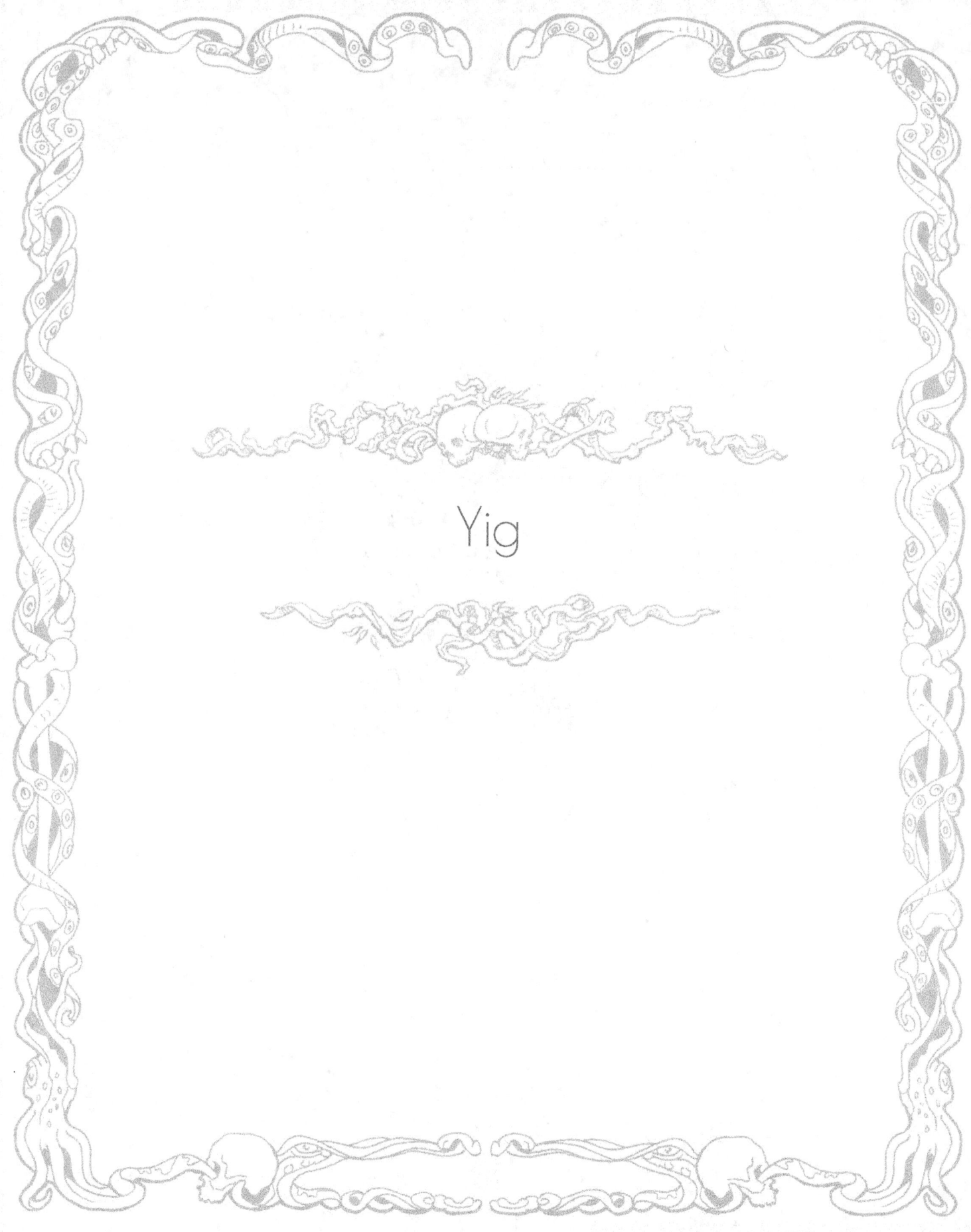

Yig

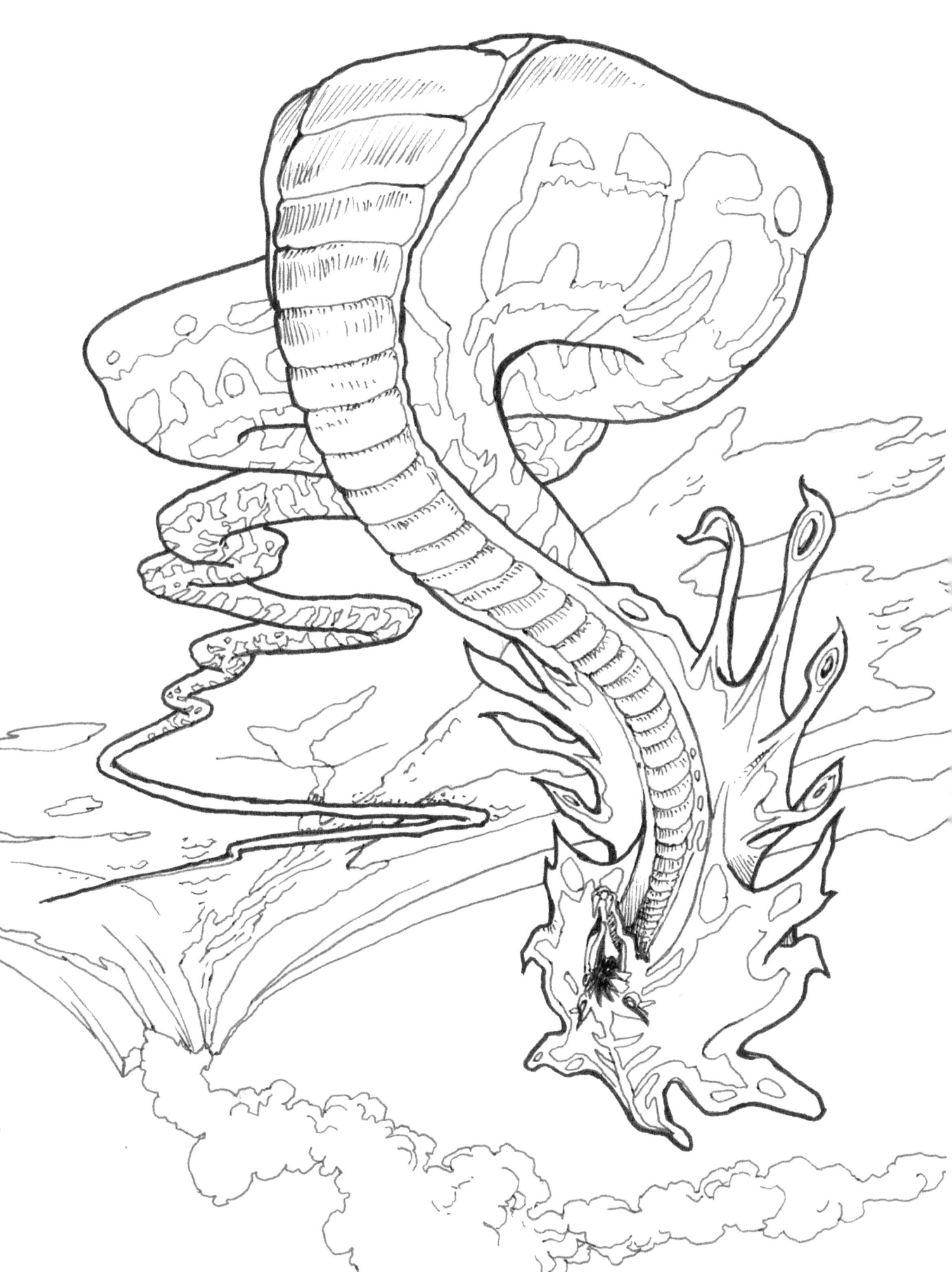

Zoog

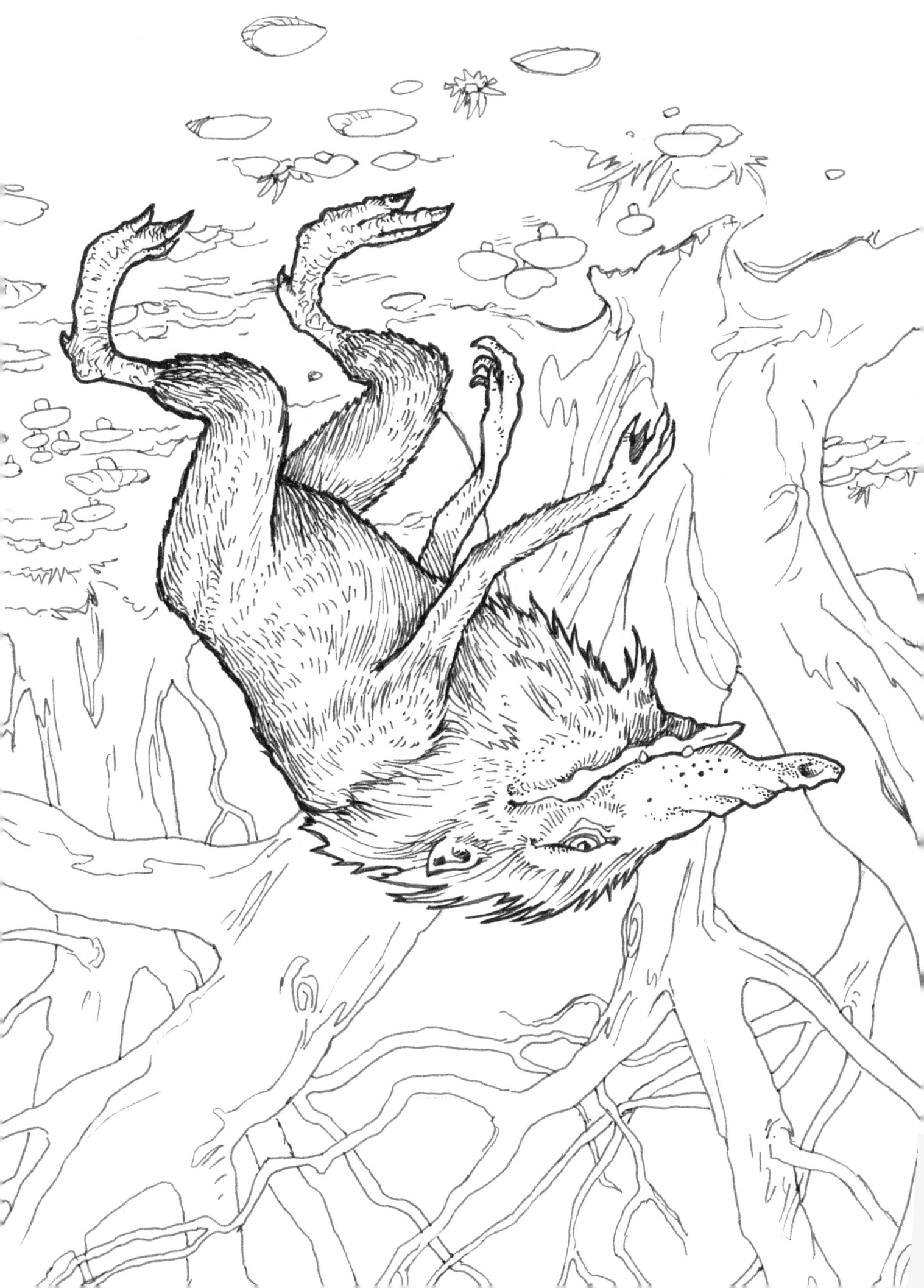